EXPLORING
ROMAN
LONDON

EXPLORING
ROMAN
LONDON

SIMON WEBB

PEN & SWORD **HISTORY**

AN IMPRINT OF PEN & SWORD BOOKS LTD.
YORKSHIRE - PHILADELPHIA

First published in Great Britain in 2023 by
Pen & Sword History
An imprint of
Pen & Sword Books Ltd
Yorkshire - Philadelphia

ISBN 978 1 39905 849 0

Typeset in INDIA by IMPEC eSolutions
Printed and bound in England by CPI Group (UK) Ltd, Croydon, CRO 4YY

Pen & Sword Books Ltd. incorporates the Imprints of Pen & Sword
Archaeology, Atlas, Aviation, Battleground, Discovery, Family History, History,
Maritime, Military, Naval, Politics, Railways, Select, Transport, True Crime,
Fiction, Frontline Books, Leo Cooper, Praetorian Press, Seaforth Publishing,
Wharncliffe, White Owl and After the Battle.

For a complete list of Pen & Sword titles please contact

PEN & SWORD BOOKS LIMITED
47 Church Street, Barnsley, South Yorkshire S70 2AS, United Kingdom
E-mail: enquiries@pen-and-sword.co.uk
Website: www.pen-and-sword.co.uk

or

PEN AND SWORD BOOKS
1950 Lawrence Rd, Havertown, PA 19083, USA
E-mail: Uspen-and-sword@casematepublishers.com
Website: www.penandswordbooks.com

Contents

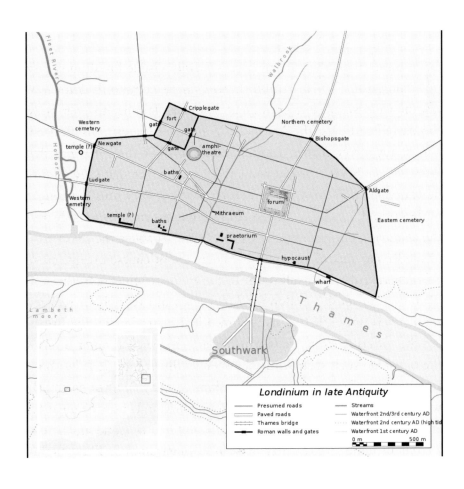

Londinium in late Antiquity

Introduction

In some cities, the ancient past is plainly visible for all to see. In Rome, the Flavian Amphitheatre, more commonly known as the Colosseum, is a prominent landmark familiar to everybody. Similarly in Athens, the Acropolis looms over the city, visible from almost any street corner. London isn't a bit like that. It is not that there are no 2,000-year-old ruins to be seen, more that they tend to be concealed and must be hunted out. Often, they must be sought underground, for the street level in London has risen inexorably over the centuries, until the modern streets are 20ft above the street level of the Roman city of Londinium. There are of course exceptions to this general rule. A 9ft-tall statue of the goddess Minerva has been in plain sight in south London for 2,000 years and yet nobody realized what it was until 2021. This is shown in Illustration 1. Then there are the towering stone walls which mark the original outer limit of the city. One such section may be seen in Illustration 2. It has been standing near Tower Hill since the third century AD, but so stoutly was it constructed that it looks as though it would easily be good for another couple of thousand years. Still in Greater London, there is a street of tombs, which may be seen in Illustration 3. These highly visible remains are, though, the exception and those wishing to explore Roman London must be prepared to both walk the streets and then dive underground into cellars and crypts when occasion demands.

A surprising amount still exists of London's first incarnation as a military encampment and then a trading centre of the Romans who occupied England for 400 years. In a way, it would be strange if this were not to be the case. After all, Roman London lasted for 400 years or

1. Greatly altered statue of the goddess Minerva.

so: the same span of time which covers the period from the coronation of the first King Charles in 1626 to that of his namesake in 2023. Such a great length of time is bound to have left its mark. Among the visible remains are a fort, more than twice as large as the better-known ones which lay along the line of Hadrian's Wall, an amphitheatre capable of seating far more people than the Albert Hall, and even the floors of domestic houses, intact in their original locations and as well preserved as anything to be found in the city of Pompeii.

Before we begin looking at Roman London though, it will be necessary to ask ourselves what was here before the arrival of the

2. Part of the Roman wall at Tower Hill.

3. Roman tombs at Keston, Greater London.

Romans. What was it about this part of the Thames Valley which caused the invading army to choose it as a base and later to build a city by the river? To understand this, we must start by studying the topography of the area as it was 2,000 years ago. Although it is not immediately apparent today, central London was once a district of rivers, islands, mudflats and marshes, parts of which were similar to the Norfolk Broads. Traces of this lost, watery landscape are still discernible beneath the heavy mantle of concrete and glass which now covers and obscures it. Finding these signs of the lost landscape of London though will entail an exploration on foot of some obscure and little-known byways of the city.

The map of Roman London at the front of this book will be useful when exploring the sites described in the text. By referring to it frequently, it should prove possible to get the 'feel' of the Roman city and make sense of its topography. It may be particularly valuable when trying to visualize the way in which vanished buildings such as the basilica and amphitheatre relate to the modern streets of the capital.

Chapter 1

London before London

Geology and geography both play a crucial role in history. England, for instance, would hardly have been the birthplace of the Industrial Revolution in the eighteenth century had there not been abundant supplies of both coal and iron ore. The fact that Britain is an island has also, of course, influenced the development of civilization, to say nothing of shaping the psyche of the British people in no small measure.

The position of London, as it relates to the wider world, is no coincidence. The city grew up in that particular part of a river valley for reasons relating both to military necessity and commercial convenience. In other words, the fact that even today London is a centre of finance and commerce is no mere chance, but derives from its geographical location. It was the Romans who were ultimately responsible for the status of London as a mercantile centre and the way in which this happened is of interest to anybody who wishes fully to understand the history of London during the Roman occupation of Britain.

Two thousand years ago, that part of the Thames Valley which we know now as London was an uninhabited area of rivers, marshes and forest. Mudflats and streams crisscrossed what would one day become the British capital and it was an uninviting place in which to live. There is no evidence of a permanent settlement there before the coming of the Romans in 43 AD. But this does not mean that nobody ever came there or that this stretch of river might not have had some significance at that time. There is strong reason to suppose that 4,500 years before the army of Claudius seized the hills of what would become central

London the Thames and its banks held some sort of mystical affinity for the tribes who roamed Britain at that time. Illustration 4 shows what the geographical layout of the London area would have been before the establishment of a city. There are a dozen rivers, all of which have now been culverted over and driven underground.

Some of these rivers had superstitious or religious significance for the inhabitants of prehistoric Britain. There are no written records from this time, of course, that is after all the very definition of prehistoric, but judging by the archaeological evidence, it looks as though the people who visited the area thought that gods and goddesses lived in the water, especially the water of the largest of the rivers, the Thames. As we shall see when we look in a later chapter about the religious practices of the Romans in London, there was a general reverence for sources of water such as wells, springs and rivers. Offerings were made to rivers and wells in the form of gifts; sometimes material possessions and also in the form of money. Curiously enough, this custom or superstition of appeasing gods in this way still lingers on in Britain to this very day.

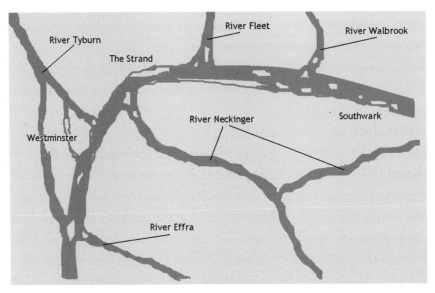

4. London in 43 AD, at the time of the Roman invasion.

In November 2006 a financial marketing agency compiled a report called the 'Fountain Money Mountain'. It was revealed that one person in five in Britain regularly throws coins into fountains, wells and other watery locations. Of course, this is simply what many people do when they pass a well or pool of water. The fountains in London's Trafalgar Square and Marble Arch accumulate coins thrown in for luck. When a public fountain or pool is designed, the throwing-in of coins by the public has to be factored into the plans. This may seem so obvious that it scarcely needs to be mentioned. However, a moment's thought will show that this is a very odd way to carry on. Why do we throw coins into wishing wells? The answer lies in the distant past and was a practice also observed by Roman Londoners.

In 1993, during a very low tide on the Thames, some ancient-looking posts were revealed as the water receded. Carbon dating showed that they dated from the Bronze Age, about 1500 BC. At first, the suggestion was made that they were part of a bridge built at that time across the river, but a more likely explanation for the structure emerged after more consideration. When the posts were erected, two spears with bronze heads had been driven deep into the mud and simply abandoned there. The wood had decayed, but the spearheads remained. Their loss was obviously deliberate and it was thought that they had been intentionally sacrificed in this way to propitiate the gods. This led to the hypothesis that the posts had been part not of a bridge, but rather a jetty. This would have jutted out into the river and perhaps ended in a platform. The purpose of this would have been to allow people to hurl valuable items into the river, in a public demonstration of their piety and devotion to the deities of the river. In case this sounds far-fetched, we recall that similar platforms have been found elsewhere. We also bear in mind the beautiful examples of helmets, shields and swords from the years before the Roman invasion which have been recovered from the Thames in pristine condition.

The La Tène culture is the name given to a particular period of Europe's Iron Age. It takes its name from a site in Switzerland, at the edge of a lake. When the water level there dropped, masses of metalwork and pieces of jewellery which had been deposited there over the years were recovered. A wooden structure was found, which had apparently been erected so that those wishing to sacrifice their goods to the gods could be sure that they would sink into the deepest water. A similar arrangement was seen at the English archaeological site of Flag Fen in Cambridgeshire. In Wales, the lake of Llyn Cerrig Bach was near an RAF airfield which was being constructed in the 1940s. The lake was partially drained as part of this work, and over a hundred swords, chains, pieces of jewellery and other items from the Bronze Age were recovered. They had been deposited there as part of ritual activity.

This kind of activity seems so strange to us that it is hardly surprising that we should assume that a series of wooden posts leading out towards the middle of a river should be part of a bridge. Why would anybody build such a thing and then stop before reaching the opposite bank? Because the Romans shared with the British Celts a common cultural heritage, derived from their Indo-European origins, it makes sense to think about this a little, because otherwise we might find it difficult to understand what the Romans were up to with the cemeteries and temples which they set up outside the gates of their cities, including of course London.

Just in front of the MI6 building on the south bank of the Thames, also near Vauxhall, some more posts were discovered and these turned out to be almost twice as old as those from the Bronze Age. They were probably about the size of telegraph poles when they were placed in prepared holes on the foreshore and might have been something along the lines of totem poles. When they were raised here, 6,500 years ago, Britain was still in the Stone Age. It is unlikely that anybody was building a house on the muddy flats which fringed the river and again, the most likely explanation is that these were part of some religious structure.

By the time that the Romans set up their first camp near here, in 43 AD, the Thames had already been the subject of religious devotion in some form or other for 4,500 years. This, and the lack of any signs of settlement along this part of the Thames, is strong evidence that the whole area may have had some religious importance to the Celts who lived in Britain when the Romans came. Perhaps there was a taboo on living too close to the river or it might also have been the border between hostile tribes. There was certainly something special about the future site of London, but we are unlikely ever to be able work out the exact nature of what it was which set it apart from the rest of the land.

The fact that both the sets of wooden remains were in the Vauxhall area, not far from Westminster, may be significant, because at Westminster, slightly upstream from where the Houses of Parliament now stand, was a ford across the river. Tracks led to this ford from both the east, from Dover, and also towards the north, in the direction of Wales. In other words, this was a place where travellers moved from one part of the country to another. Perhaps it was neutral ground or possibly a place regarded as being special in some way, so that people would pass through it, but not linger; certainly not build their huts there.

Of course, there were also practical reasons which tended to make this an unattractive place to live permanently. The Thames was as much as four times as wide as it is now and it was fed by various rivers, which cut the land here into separate areas. At Westminster and Vauxhall, the Tyburn flowed from the north and divided into a delta roughly where Buckingham Palace is today. The two branches then flowed south and entered the Thames, one at Westminster and the other at Vauxhall. This had the effect of creating an island which, because it was low lying and surrounded by water, was swampy and waterlogged. As late as the medieval period, it was known as Bulinga Fen and later by the name of Thorney Island. On the other side of the Thames, the Effra also formed a delta at roughly the same point. There were other rivers flowing into the Thames in this area, such as the Westbourne, the Fleet and the Walbrook in the north, and the Neckinger and Falcon Brook in the south.

The whole area of what is now central London, from Vauxhall to the Tower of London, was largely a marshy, sodden wasteland, wholly unsuited either to live in or for agricultural use. Travelling around it meant wading across rivers and streams and in some parts, Southwark for instance, the land consisted of just an archipelago of small islands, separated by mudflats at low tide and deep water when the tide was in. This whole desolate place was not an attractive prospect when it came to building a village, but was seemingly of importance as a ritual landscape. People came here to sacrifice and bury their dead, but it held nothing much of interest to the living.

There is one final point to be made about the way in which geology and geography conspired together to shape the city which was founded in this uninviting spot. The nature and appearance of a city is often a product of its location and underlying geology. In other words, people tend to build with what they can lay their hands on. Those living in the Siberian tundra at the time that the hunting of mammoths was a popular means of finding food, discovered after a while that the place was littered with the bones of those mighty beasts, but not much else. There were no forests to chop down for trees, for example. So it was that they built their huts from the bones of mammoths. In the Arctic, there is always a plentiful supply of ice and snow. This is why the Inuit built their igloos of these materials. Some cities grew up in areas where there was a ready supply of easily quarried stone and this left us with such wonders as Athens' Acropolis, which is still standing above the city 2,500 years after it was created. London has always been in rather a different position.

Beneath London lies nothing more substantial than mud and clay. There are a few chalk uplands around Greenwich, but that's it as far as stone is concerned. In the English country of Cornwall, there still survives an entire Iron Age village called Chysauster. This consists of stone-built houses which date from about 100 BC. Cornwall has of course a good deal of rock beneath it, with reefs breaking the surface and providing an easily accessible source of building material. The houses at Chysauster are still standing after 2,000 years. London was less fortunate. Wood, mud and clay are nowhere near as durable as granite, which is why the first incarnation of the city was so easily destroyed by the army led by Boudicca in 60 AD. The whole place was burned to the ground quite easily.

Later on, it is true, the Romans built in stone, but this had to be transported all the way from Maidstone in Kent to London. This naturally restricted the number of stone buildings seen in ancient London. We see today in the capital many houses, shops and public buildings which have been built of brick, but not quite as many made out of stone. Scottish cities like Aberdeen and Welsh cities like Brecon have always been able to construct even workers' cottages from stone, because they have so much available locally.

We have seen in this chapter why nobody was living permanently in that part of the country where the Romans would choose to set up a base which would, in the course of time, become a great city. Whatever the disadvantage deterring the Celts living in the country at that time from settling there, none of them were sufficiently strong to discourage the invaders. Indeed, they spotted geographical points which, in their eyes, militated in favour of this being an eminently suitable spot to establish a city. Not least of these was that looked at in a wider, European perspective, that very swampy and deserted piece of land could be a most desirable place for trade, that is to say importing and exporting goods by ship. The Rhine faces the Thames across the North Sea and the tidal part of the Thames reached inland as far as Westminster. This meant that ships sailing from central Europe could be borne up the River Thames on the tide, ending up where the new Roman port was to be. London might have been a pretty hopeless site for agriculture, but it was ideally suited for commerce and trade.

All this though lay in the future when the Roman legions landed in Britain in 43 AD, with the aim of conquering the island and turning it into a province of the Empire. It was quite another chance of geography which led the invaders first to establish a camp in the area.

Chapter 2

The Founding of a City

As every schoolchild once knew, Julius Caesar invaded Britain in 55 BC. He did not stay long though and after having a good look round, he sailed back to Gaul. Caesar returned the following year and fought a battle or two, before once again retreating to Gaul, leaving the British to their own devices for the next century or so. It was to be another 97 years before the real Roman invasion of Britain was launched. In 43 AD the emperor Claudius ordered his army to conquer Britain. He had several good reasons for undertaking such a venture. Having been unexpectedly installed as emperor following the assassination of his nephew Caligula, Claudius knew that he needed to make his mark and establish his authority, particularly over the army. There were those in Rome who viewed him as a weak man and it was vital to dispel such an idea.

Invading and occupying Britain solved two problems at once for the new emperor. In the first place it would show that he was bold enough to undertake a project at which even the great Julius Caesar had failed, the conquest of a territory on the frontier of the known world. Secondly, it would keep the army busy and away from Rome. It had been soldiers who had murdered his nephew and Claudius thought that it would be well to keep the army busy in another part of the world, rather than leave them sitting around in Rome with the leisure to plot further assassinations. At least 40,000 men would be needed to subdue Britain and these soldiers at least would not have the time to be conspiring at his overthrow or murder.

There was another good reason for deciding to invade and occupy the island of Britain and this was that it looked as though it might make sound economic sense to do so. According to the Greek geographer Strabo, writing a few years before Claudius launched his invasion, this is what Britain was like at that time;

> Most of the island is flat and overgrown with forests, although many of its districts are hilly. It bears grain, cattle, gold, silver, and iron. These things, accordingly, are exported from the island, as also hides, and slaves, and dogs that are by nature suited to the purposes of the chase; the Celti, however, use both these and the native dogs for the purposes of war too.

There has probably never been the ruler of an empire yet who was not affected by hearing that a small country on the edge of his empire was full of silver and gold. Claudius was no exception to this general rule, and it must have looked to him, when he was weighing the matter up in his mind, that at the very least the invasion would pay for itself. Who knew, it might even become a profitable venture which would ultimately enrich Rome.

The most important settlement in Britain at the time that a Roman army arrived on the coast of Kent in 43 AD was Camulodunum, which now lies buried beneath modern Colchester. To get there from the landing site in Kent, the army would have to cross the Thames and head north. It would first be necessary to march west though, until a spot might be found where the river could be forded. The closest such point was in the area which is now central London, most probably near the present-day Westminster Bridge.

There is, as we have noted, no evidence that anybody was at that time living in what was soon to become the Roman city of Londinium. The Thames was a natural border between the tribes of the Catevallauni in the north and the Atrebates and Cantiaci in the south. As such, the river and the areas around its banks were very likely viewed as neutral territory, a no man's land, if you like. Then too, there is reason to suppose that the Thames had some kind of religious or spiritual significance to the people living in southern Britain, because of certain prehistoric remains found nearby, and this too might have meant that there was a taboo against actually living on the banks of the river. As far as we know, it was the Romans who first decided to settle permanently and make their home in that part of the Thames Valley. Their reason for doing so was, at least to begin with, purely military. It would have been necessary to secure a crossing point so that the troops were able to pass freely from one side of the river to the other, without having to fight their way up the opposite shore each time they wished to head north. The matter of where the Romans should set up their first stronghold though was complicated by the natural features of the land surrounding the ford across the Thames. This is another aspect of something discussed in the previous chapter, the way in which geography and geology dictated both the location, and subsequent development, of London.

In modern London, only one river is usually visible and that is of course the Thames. It is clearly defined and its shoreline delineated by stone walls, which prevent it escaping its confines. Walking in central London today, one can be quite confident about the whereabouts of open water and the only bridges one might need to cross are those from the south side of the river to the north bank. It was not always so. Two thousand years ago, this part of England was a network of rivers and streams which ran through marshes and around islands. Here and there were low hills, rising 30 or 40ft above the surface of the nearby rivers. It was a desolate and bleak place, inhabited only by frogs, rats, mice and waterbirds, and it would be hard to imagine a less inviting spot to start a city. There were certainly drier and more attractive spots along the banks of the Thames than this, but there was that important point that the most easterly ford across the Thames lay in the vicinity. Before we consider this question in detail, perhaps it might be interesting to look with fresh eyes at the centre of London and try and discover what it would have looked like in those days, before anybody lived there. What happened to all these rivers, marshes and hills? After all, central London these days seems to be as flat as a pancake and dry as a bone. Illustration 4 (see page 2) shows what the area around London's financial district in the north and Southwark to the south would have looked like at that time. As will be seen, it is a network of islands and streams.

The Thames was far wider and shallower than it is today. It was a sluggish river too, and rose and fell with the tide much less than is now the case. Other rivers flowed into the Thames and between these rivers the land was often marshy and waterlogged. The situation was even less inviting around that part of the river which could be forded. Three rivers entered the Thames at that point and where the Houses of Parliament stand today was an island, surrounded by two branches of the River Tyburn. Nobody wishes to camp in a swamp and the first permanent camp would therefore have to be a little way from this ford and preferably on a piece of land which remained dry, even at high tide. It is time to examine the highest hill in central London, where the first incarnation of Londinium was established a few years after the invasion of Britain in 43 AD.

We begin our exploration of Roman London by taking the London Underground's Central Line to Bank station and then leaving the station by Exit 3. We emerge in front of a classical-looking building fronted by fluted columns in the Greek style. This is the Royal Exchange. If we look around us, the landscape could scarcely look flatter, with no suggestion at all of any hills to be seen. As a matter of fact, we are now standing at the bottom of a valley, with a river still flowing beneath the Bank of England, the building we can see if we turn to our left. This area lay between the two hills upon which London was founded. Of the first settlement, the city which sprang up on a nearby hill, nothing at all remains to be seen. It was burned to the ground by Boudicca and her army in 60 AD and remains now only as a deposit of burnt clay and charred wood, which archaeologists call the 'Red Layer'. Digging down 20ft in the City of London or Southwark, on the other side of the Thames, will reveal evidence of the holocaust which overcame the first incarnation of Roman London.

We are more concerned with what may still be seen of Londinium though, the city which rose from the ashes of that first great fire of London. If we walk towards the Royal Exchange and then veer right, we will find ourselves walking up a street called Cornhill. Cross the road and carry on up the slight incline. As we walk along, a careful observation of the buildings on either side of the street will show that this is a hill, although one with a very gentle gradient; so much so that it is almost imperceptible. However, looking at the doorways, steps and gratings set in the walls of the buildings as we pass along the thoroughfare, it will be observed that they are at a very slight angle to the pavement. This is the only clue that we are in fact walking uphill. This is the highest hill in the City of London and it forms part of a low terrace which overlooked the river. A stream divided the little plateau in two; the Walbrook, from whose valley we started. Although it is invisible today, it still flows beneath the streets and we shall see later where it meets the Thames.

After about 250 yards, we reach an alleyway on the right called St Peter's Alley. If we enter this alleyway, we will find ourselves in what must surely rank as one of the drabbest and least inviting gardens in London. This is the churchyard of St Peter's church and when we walk into this shady spot, with its stunted yew trees, we are standing on the highest point in the City of London, that is to say the area which is roughly where Londinium was founded. We are now 58ft above sea level. Of course, this hill has grown since the Romans were here; it is now about 20ft higher than it was at that time. What has caused this growth? Is it the movement of some tectonic plates which have caused the centre of London to rise up in this way, much as the Himalayas are growing as one of the Earth's plates collides with another? In fact, the explanation for the increase in height is a good deal more interesting than that.

In the Middle East, some mounds like small hills are called tels. Illustration 5 shows us such a place. This is Tel Ubedieya, on the

5. Archaeological mound in the Jordan Valley.

banks of the River Jordan in Israel. It appears to be a low hill, but this area of the Jordan Valley is quite flat. What we are seeing is the accumulated debris of millennia. For thousands of years, houses and huts have been built here from mud, wood and stone. As one of these building collapsed or was demolished, the remains were used as the foundation for the next home erected on the site. In this way, little by little, the ground level rose. Some such archaeological mounds are very high, for example that at Jericho, near the Dead Sea. In central London the street level is, in consequence of this process, about 20ft higher than it was 2,000 years ago. This is why the best-preserved Roman remains are today to be found in cellars and crypts. We shall soon be looking at just such a piece of ancient London which may be found only a few yards from here.

This then is where the invaders built their first army camp. It was dry and from the top of this hill, the soldiers would have had a good view of the surrounding country. It was a good defensive position too, because of course attackers would be coming uphill towards the defenders. The hills of Cornhill and Ludgate are really one plateau, divided in two by a small river which we now know as the Walbrook. This high ground is made up largely of gravel which was deposited here during the last Ice Age and this means that the land does not become waterlogged. It was a perfect location for a first base and to secure a crossing place on the Thames. To the west, the hill of Ludgate, where St Paul's Cathedral stands today, was guarded by the River Fleet, which was a fast-flowing and quite substantial river at that time. To the south was the Thames and anybody attacking from that direction would have to cross the river and then charge uphill at the defenders; not an enticing prospect from a tactical point of view. Then too, even at high tide, the River Thames did not reach as high as this hilltop.

It was considerations such as those listed above which made this the logical spot for the Romans to choose for the first permanent settlement in this part of the Thames Valley. The evidence suggests though that this did not happen for another six or seven years. That the army had marching camps here to secure the river crossing is logical, but no civilians seemed to have felt inclined to make their homes here for the first few years after the invasion.

With a force on the other side of the river, where modern-day Southwark now lies, the army had a secure crossing point which would, in the fullness of time, be where London's first bridge would be built. It may be assumed that traders and camp-followers were gradually attracted to the army base, with a view to making money. Who were these people? Some were probably Celts who thought that there might be money to be made. Women willing to sell their bodies, men offering to act as interpreters and so on. Then too, word would soon spread back to mainland Europe that there might be profitable business in supplying the soldiers based in this remote and inhospitable territory with goods which were unavailable locally. Wine, different kinds of food from their boring rations, gaming pieces, dice, warm clothes and the hundred and one other things which traders have always been keen to supply to an army stationed in an inhospitable foreign country. It is impossible to say under what conditions such people lived, whether in tents or hastily-constructed shacks, but we might guess that over the first few years after the Roman army settled here, some kind of shanty town grew up around their camp. At any rate, by 50 AD there was, if not a city, then at least a village or small town on the top of Cornhill and Ludgate Hill.

It is impossible to say how many people were living in Londinium in 50 AD, or ten years later, when disaster befell the city. The story of Boudicca and her destruction of London is too well known to need repeating in detail. Boudicca was a queen of the Iceni in East Anglia and she and her daughters were shockingly treated by the Romans. She was flogged and both her daughters raped when she fell out with the Roman authorities. Her revenge was memorable. She gathered an army and then swept south to Colchester, which by that time was a Roman city which had replaced the Celtic Camulodunum. The city was put to the torch and the inhabitants massacred. Following this victory, Boudicca and her forces headed for Londinium. Illustration 6

6. Statue of Queen Boudicca, who destroyed Londinium.

shows an imaginative Victorian idea of how the Iceni queen would have looked in her chariot. The Roman army had realized that the place was indefensible and so had retreated, leaving the city open. Boudicca's army dealt with it just as that had Colchester. Every inhabitant, Roman and Celtic, on whom they could lay their hands was slaughtered, often in the most savage way imaginable. Some Roman noblewomen were captured and they were impaled on stakes, their breasts being cut off and then sewn to their mouths, as though they were eating them. Following this, the whole place was burned down.

Only archaeologists ever get to see the remains of the city which Boudicca sacked. The 'Red Layer', as it is known, covers the whole of where we are now standing on Cornhill and is also found across the river in Southwark. It is simply a mass of charred wood and burnt clay. By the time that Boudicca had finished with the place, it must have looked like the aftermath of Hiroshima, with nothing at all to indicate that a city had once stood here. As far as the eye could see, there was just a smoking plain of ash. As was remarked earlier, little remains of that first iteration of the city. However, there are traces to be found of later buildings, those erected in the heyday of Londinium. Following her success here, Boudicca of course went north and repeated the process on Verulamium, which is today known as St Albans.

If there was no pre-existing settlement here, then what is the origin of the modern name of the city? Why is it called London? The Roman name for the camp which they established here, and which later became a city, was Londinium. They did not pluck this name out of thin air though; it was almost certainly based upon a Celtic name for this part for the Thames Valley. It has variously been suggested that the word 'London' is related to the Celtic for 'dark river' or 'black pool'. Others suggest that its derivation is older than that and that it is based upon some expression in an earlier Indo-European language, and is connected with the words for 'swimming' and 'river'. The truth is, we are never likely to be able to settle this particular question for good.

About the name of the river which flows through the heart of London, we may be sure that its name long predates the foundation of the Roman city. In *The Gallic War*, Julius Caesar refers to crossing the Tamesis. It has been speculated that this name comes from a combination of two Celtic words; *tam*, meaning wide, and *uisghe*, which means water. The name of the Thames has always been pronounced with an initial 'T', rather than 'Th'. In the sixteenth century, some English scholars decided that spelling the river 'Thames', rather than 'Tames' as it was at that time, would look a little more classical and the habit has stuck.

At any rate, the city rose again, this time to be a more solid and substantial place, with buildings and walls so stoutly made that parts of them can still be seen thousands of years later. After a permanent army base had been set up near here, the new city was built. Unlike the old one, which had been somewhat haphazard, this was to be a planned settlement, with grand buildings in the proper Roman style. Before, people seemingly built houses wherever they pleased, but now a definite structure was imposed upon the area, with official buildings and an arrangement of streets which was dictated to those who wished to live there. Like any important Roman city, the heart of Londinium was to be a basilica and forum.

Returning now to the place where we are currently standing, this was once Londinium's basilica. It was the centre of the city's civil administration, something like a town hall, offices of the civil service and law courts all combined. It was built here, on the highest point of London, so that it could be seen from all around, a little like the castles which were later erected by the Normans after they in turn invaded the country. The Romans wanted to make sure that everybody could see at a glance this symbol of Roman civilization. The first basilica was built here a few years after the city was destroyed by Boudicca's army, but after only a decade or two, it was demolished to make way for a much larger and grander basilica and forum. This new complex, which was completed before the end of the first century AD, consisted of an enormous basilica which was over 450ft long. Adjoining it was a public square, the forum. This was partly a market and also somewhere people simply met and talked. It was a place too where orators could deliver public speeches. Perhaps the closest equivalent today might be London's Trafalgar Square.

It is time to consider a theme which will crop up often in this book, which is the way in which the Roman history of the city still has, to this very day, a profound effect upon modern London. Take the church in whose grounds we are standing. This is reputed to be the most ancient church in London. Not, that is to say, the fabric of the present building, but rather the location. There have been earlier churches on this spot and the first was almost certainly erected on the ruins of the Roman basilica. The alignment of the walls of St Peter's follow very closely the line of the basilica and it is stands in the position in the basilica where some basilicas in other cities had shrines or pagan temples. Given Christianity's history in Britain of appropriating sites connected with earlier religions and erecting their own churches upon them, this may be significant.

Leaving the churchyard and continuing along the alley through which we have been walking will bring us out into Gracechurch Street. Facing us on the opposite side of the road is a cavernous archway which leads into Leadenhall Market. This too may be an example of the continuation of the use of a London location over the centuries and millennia. The arcades and cobbled alleyways of the market we see today date only from the late nineteenth century; it is an entirely Victorian creation. However, there has been a market on this spot since at least the fourteenth century and quite possibly even earlier than that. The area to the right, including that covered by the market, was part of the Roman forum which, as we know, was partly a market, with stalls selling all kinds of wares. It may be that a market of some kind has been here for 2,000 years.

If we cross Gracechurch Street, we can get a better look at Leadenhall Market, which has for many people, even those who have never been here in their lives, an eerie familiarity. This is because it stood in for Diagon Alley in the first of the Harry Potter films, *Harry Potter and the Philosopher's Stone*. This is though, by the by. Our real purpose in crossing the road is to see the last remaining visible fragment of the vast Roman basilica, which was at the time of the Roman Empire the largest building north of the Alps. We are about to view the only part of the basilica and forum which is still visible. On the left, before you enter the main part of the market, is a hairdressers called Nicholson and Griffin, which sounds like a firm of lawyers from one of Charles Dickens' novels. In the basement of this shop, which is at the street level of the Roman city, is part of the wall of the basilica. Opening a glass door there and stepping through it is like using a time machine and passing through a portal to the distant past. Illustration 7 shows this strange relic of another era. On a massive stone base are courses of bricks and the whole thing is so remarkably solid that one

7. Part of London's basilica, preserved in a modern shop.

wonders how an entire building, one which was 450ft long and built in such a way, could simply have vanished, leaving behind only this trace of its former existence.

As a matter of fact, the basilica and forum have not altogether vanished, it is just that we are no longer able to see them. The foundations of Leadenhall Market, when it was being built, were not enormously deep and it was not necessary to remove all the stonework which lay beneath them. This explains the survival of the fragment of pier at which we have been looking. In 1986, the Museum of London conducted extensive work when the foundations for a new building were being dug in the area. It was discovered that the concrete foundations of the basilica still existed in many areas. When telephone lines were being laid around Cornhill, the same thing was found, that the foundations of the basilica were largely intact.

Leaving Nicholson and Griffin, we turn left and walk down Gracechurch Street until we come to Fenchurch Street on our left. Here too is another example of the way in which the fabric of Roman London is still visible in the modern city. It will be observed that Fenchurch Street curves away to the left out of sight. In the same way, the street which it becomes as it approaches the Bank of England, Lombard Street, also forms part of the same curve. These streets were laid down during the Anglo-Saxon era, when a road was constructed leading from one end of the old walled city to the other. Fenchurch Street begins at Aldgate, which was one of the gates through the Roman walls. The road which eventually became these two streets did not travel in a straight line through the ruins of the Roman city, but curved around the southern end of the forum. As you look up Fenchurch Street from this point, the buildings on the left mark the line of the forum. Illustration 8 shows a model of the forum and basilica as it would have appeared from Gracechurch Street. To the right in this picture, Fenchurch Street curves away, and to the left Lombard Street. The entrance to the forum would have been right

8. The forum and basilica, as seen from present-day Gracechurch Street.

where we are now standing, where Gracechurch Street cuts across those other two thoroughfares.

We cannot know at this late date whether avoiding the remains of the forum was caused by some taboo or superstitious dread of such a large construction, or whether the motive was more practical and it was simply easier to route the road around the forum rather than going to all the trouble of demolishing the surviving part of it so that the road could pass across the site. Looking down Fenchurch Street, we are looking at the location when a Roman fort was built soon after the Boudiccan destruction of the city. We walk back now along Lombard Street towards Bank Tube station, where we began our walk.

From Bank, we are going to trace the course of the lost river of the Walbrook, which was important in Roman London as a source of fresh water. It bisected the city. We have been walking along the left-hand side of Lombard Street in the direction of Bank. When we reach what seems to be the end of the street, cross over and keep walking along, heading to the right. We come to the area of the Bank of England, which we will see to our right. A number of streets meet here. We keep walking and veer left, passing the Mansion House on our left. This imposing building, with a classical façade fronted, like the Royal Exchange, with the sort of columns one might expect to see on the Parthenon, is the official residence of the Lord Mayor of London. By the side of the Mansion House, once we have just passed it, is a street called Walbrook. This, unsurprisingly, is named after the river, whose course it follows. Turn left and walk down Walbrook.

On the right is a site which we shall be learning about in a later chapter. This is the temple dedicated to the Persian god Mithras, which once stood on the banks of the Walbrook. Continuing down the street will bring us to Cannon Street Station, the entrance to which may be seen across the road to the left. Work began on constructing Cannon Street in 1863 and it was soon found that the site chosen had at one time been an immense Roman building, with extensive gardens and pools. It has subsequently been suggested by archaeologists that this might perhaps have been the official residence of the governor of the province of Britannia. It was certainly grand enough and it was difficult to imagine a private individual having such a vast property in the centre of the city.

More recently, doubt has been expressed about the precise nature of the building which lies buried under Cannon Street Station. From time to time, during the erection of new buildings, the remains of walls are uncovered, but there has been no definitive evidence that this really was where the governor was based. There is though, a tantalizing clue. Although all the remains of what is usually termed the 'palace' are deep underground and not accessible to view, there is one fragment on display which we can see.

If we turn left and walk up Cannon Street, we shall soon come to one of the most curious archaeological remains in the capital. Protruding a little from the wall of 111 Cannon Street is a stone structure with a glass window set into it. Through this may be glimpsed a grimy chunk of grey stone which is not much larger than the average microwave oven. This is the London Stone, and its recorded history goes back a thousand years. Its actual origin though and arrival in this part of London probably occurred twice as long ago. A few years ago, when rebuilding work was taking place, the stone was removed from its present location and displayed for a while at the Museum of London. Illustration 9 shows what it looks like today.

The stone which we can see through the pane of glass is limestone, most probably quarried in the English country of Rutland, and it is only a smaller part of what was once a very large and substantial

9. The London Stone.

monolith which stood on the other side of the road, where Cannon Street Station now stands. There are several references to the stone from the late Tudor period and it was so well-known at that time that when Shakespeare introduced it into one of his plays, he had no need to explain to the audience the significance of the London Stone. At the end of the sixteenth century, scholar John Stow referred to it in these terms;

> A great stone pitched upright on the south side of Cannon Street, fixed in the ground verie deepe, fastened with bars of iron, and otherwise so strongly set, that if Cartes do run against it by negligence, the wheeles be broken, and the stone itself unshaken.

It is plain that at one time there was a lot more of this stone than we can today see tucked into that little hole in the front of a building.

The London Stone originally stood on the other side of the road, right where Cannon Street Station is and it was, from at least the Middle Ages onwards, thought that it conveyed some kind of spiritual or supernatural power. When, in 1450, a man called Jack Cade led a rebellion in which he tried to seize London, one of his first acts on entering the city with his men was to strike the London Stone with his sword, in this way claiming authority over the entire city. Shakespeare describes this event in *Henry VI Part 2*.

The discovery of what might well be the palace of the Roman governor of Britain, which stood, as we know, roughly where Cannon Street Station is now, caused speculation that the London Stone might be a Roman relic. For some time, it was asserted that it could be a Roman milestone which marked the centre of the capital and from which all distances to outlying regions was measured. This was an interesting theory, although one with little evidence to back it up. Current thinking is that it is more likely that it was part of the structure of the building itself or perhaps a gatepost. If the building was indeed the official residence of the most important official in Britain during the Roman occupation, then a superstitious reverence might have arisen for the site over the four centuries or so that Londinium was a Roman city. This awe of the power which the palace represented might have lingered on as a folk memory, even after the palace itself was gone. In this way, the feeling might have been transferred to the one remaining part of the complex of buildings; a gatepost which somehow survived even after all the rest of the building had been swept away by the tide of time.

Admittedly, this theory can never be proved, but both the material of which the London Stone is made and its original position in Cannon Street make it the most likely one. It is certainly a good deal more plausible than some of the more recent ideas, such as that this was the stone from which King Arthur drew the sword Excalibur, to prove himself the true king!

If we now cross over the road to Cannon Street Station and look back along the way we have been walking, we see at once the dip in the road which shows us the valley of the Walbrook. This perspective can be seen in Illustration 10 overleaf and it is obvious that we are looking at a shallow valley. The road goes gently downhill to the junction of Cannon Street and Walbrook, when it begins to slope upwards again. Even the steps leading into the railway station have had to be adjusted to compensate for this slope, as we shall see when we pass it, walking downhill towards the course of the Walbrook once more. Once we reach the first turning on our left, we pause to look around. Looking down the turning on our left, Dowgate Hill, it is immediately apparent that it *is* a hill. That's why the Walbrook ran in this direction, down to the Thames. Glancing back up Walbrook, it is possible to see that this is part of the same hill. We are afforded a perfect opportunity to see how the two chief hills of London, Cornhill and Ludgate, were divided by this little river.

Walking down Dowgate Hill, with the railway station on our left, we come to Upper Thames Street. This is what was once the riverbank.

10. The valley of the Walbrook.

From here on, the ground upon which we will be walking has been reclaimed from the Thames. Imagine as you stand here that in Roman times, the river would be right in front of you. The palatial building which may have housed the governor of the province is on your left and to your right, the Walbrook flows into the Thames.

Crossing the road, we continue in the same direction, along Cousin Lane. This will lead us after a couple of hundred yards to the Thames itself. Right in front is a short flight of steps which lead over the embankment and down to the Thames foreshore. If the tide is out, then it is possible to climb up those steps and then down on the other side. You will now be standing on a beach. The first thing to strike one's eye will be the countless fragments of red-brown tiles which lay scattered wherever you look. These are especially concentrated in spots such as this, which were once near large Roman buildings, and the reason is obvious; many of these fragments are actually broken roof tiles and building materials from the palace which we have passed. Of course, fired clay of that kind has been used by many others since the days when Londinium fell into decay, but it is possible to find pieces of fluted roof tiles which are without doubt Roman and were once part of the roof of the grand building in Cannon Street.

Readers who wish to indulge in a little amateur archaeology may at this point start picking up and examining the various fragments of tiles which they find littering the foreshore beneath the bridge leading from Cannon Street Station. Those of Roman origin are not hard to distinguish. Roof tiles used in Londinium may still be seen today in modern Rome. Two kinds are used. One is the *tegula*, which is a flat tile with flanges on two sides jutting up at right-angles to the body of the tile. These fit side by side and the gaps which are formed by the two flanges are covered by semi-circular tiles, each of which is called an *imbrex*.

After almost 2,000 years, it is scarcely surprising that most of the Roman tiles found in the river have been broken or eroded, but here and there one may still find pieces which are quite distinctive. In Illustration 11 may be seen two pieces of tiles which show clearly the

11. Roman tiles, found on the Thames foreshore.

flat part of the tile and the flange at the side. These were unearthed in the course of no more than a cursory search lasting ten minutes or so beneath the railway bridge at this part of the foreshore. It is entirely possible, even probable, given the location, that they are from the roof of what is often assumed to be the governor's palace.

If anybody wishes to see the sad remains of the Walbrook, they may do so at low tide by turning right and then walking past a large and permanently moored barge. They will come to a circular metal plate set into the concrete wall which confines the Thames to its proper place. This is the outlet for the storm drain into which the Walbrook has now been converted and after very rainy weather, one can see a trickle of water emerging and draining into the Thames.

While we are standing on the Thames foreshore, it might be worth thinking about another reason that this part of Britain was in some ways ideal as both a military and later commercial centre for the Romans. Landing from ships on the coast of Kent entails a long trek across country, before one is able to gain access to the rest of the country. Even at a smart pace of 20 or 30 miles a day, an army would still take three days to reach the Thames. Although the Thames was not tidal for as much of its length as is now the case, it *was* tidal as far as that sharp bend in the river where the Palace of Westminster is now to be found. Ships from the Continent could sail up the river on the tide and then anchor in what is now central London.

This ability to sail to the heart of Britain in that way also came in useful when Londinium became a centre for import and export. Rather than carry goods all that distance overland and then ship them across the Channel, it was possible for vessels to move easily along the Thames, across the North Sea and up the Rhine, which enters the sea in what is now the Netherlands. From there, it was, as they say, plain sailing to Mainz, where the Romans had a port. In this way, goods were shipped from the Roman Empire to Britain, and exports from Britain were able to be carried swiftly to the heart of Europe.

It is time to explore the other of those first hills upon which the Romans founded their city, although some readers may wish to save this expedition for another day. So, we can retrace our steps to Bank Tube station and either return home or, if we wish, take the Underground to the next westbound stop, which is St Paul's.

Chapter 3

Ludgate Hill and the River Fleet

If you take the London Underground's Central Line to St Paul's Station, you will find yourself practically on the doorstep of one of the world's most famous cathedrals. Looking around outside the station, it has to be said that this does not feel very much like standing on the top of a hill, but if you turn left you will see a curious plaque attached to the wall of a coffee shop. Nobody quite knows why this was made or what it represents, but it is known as the Panyer Boy. It has been in this area for 350 years and as buildings to which it was attached have been demolished, so it has been placed on whatever is then erected on the site. The inscription, which may be seen in Illustration 12, reads,

> When you have sought the citty round,
> Yet still this is the highest ground
> August the 27 1688

As it happens, laser-assisted surveying equipment and other up-to-date technology show this claim to be slightly inaccurate. Ludgate Hill, upon which you are standing, is in fact a couple of feet lower than Cornhill which lies a little to the east.

Turn your back on the Panyer Boy and walk past the entrance to the Tube station to your right. Follow the road round to the right and it is possible to see the great creamy bulk of the cathedral to your right. It dominates this area. Cross the road and walk along New Change Lane, keeping the cathedral to your right, until you come to Cannon Street. Just before you do so, you will pass on your left a paved path which leads to a short stretch of road called Watling

12. Inscription at the top of Ludgate Hill.

Street. This gives us a clue about the past, because Watling Street passed through Londinium and left it, heading west, towards Marble Arch. Cross the road and turn left in Cannon Street and then, almost immediately, turn right into Friday Street. At the end of this very short thoroughfare, you will see over to your left and on the other side of the road some brick pillars supporting wooden beams and climbing plants. This marks the entrance to one of the most curious little spots in this part of the city. Crossing the road, you will find before you a very strange sight; namely a terraced Italianate garden which has been constructed on the side of a hill. You are standing now on the crest of a hill, looking down towards the River Thames, which is obscured by ugly modern office blocks. Illustration 13 shows the view from the top of the hill. This garden, the Cleary Garden, was planted on the site of a Second World War bombsite. It is possible that some readers

13. The Cleary Garden, site of a Roman bathhouse.

will not be familiar with the expression 'bombsite' and since we shall be visiting another bombsite in the course of our explorations, a few words on the subject might not come amiss.

Between 1940 and 1945, London was subjected to ferocious pounding by bombs, cruise missiles and rockets. The explosions caused by these German munitions reduced large swathes of central London to rubble. Once this was cleared away, an empty hole showed where a building had once stood. These open spaces, many of which remained derelict throughout the 1950s and 1960s, were known as bombsites, and in the suburbs were popular playgrounds for children. Central London was covered in bombsites and although the war wrought terrible damage to the fabric of the city, it was not an unalloyed disaster. Indeed, without the Blitz, many of the Roman remains at which we shall be looking would not be visible today. They had been concealed beneath buildings for centuries and it was only the sudden blasting away of the bricks and mortar which hid them from sight which has made it possible to see so much of the past history of London today. The Cleary Garden is a perfect illustration of this.

Until the Second World War, the area leading down the hillside was a jumble of Victorian and Georgian buildings, offices and shops which had been built close to each other and huddled together down towards the river. They were all destroyed by enemy action, leaving their cellars exposed to the open air. An office worker called Joseph Brandis, who commuted into the city each day from Walthamstow, decided that the bombsite would be greatly improved by some flowers and so cleared the area of rubble and began carrying bags of mud up the hill from the Thames foreshore to make some flowerbeds. Then he brought plants from his back garden and established a pretty little oasis on what had been a cluster of ruins. It was so successful that in 1949 Queen Elizabeth (later the Queen Mother) paid a visit and congratulated Brandis on what he had managed to achieve. It is something of an injustice that the garden should have been named not after Joseph Brandis, the man who conceived the idea and brought it into being, but rather after Fred Cleary, who worked for the Corporation of the City of London's Trees Gardens and Open Spaces Committee and the Metropolitan Public Gardens Association.

Fifteen years after this little garden received a royal endorsement, a remarkable discovery was made at the bottom of the hill. In 1964, those clearing away part of an old cellar discovered some Roman walls. These turned out to have been part of a large bathhouse. It is time to look at our first Roman remains.

In a later chapter, we shall be looking in detail at the Roman bathhouses unearthed in central London, but for the present we need only know that 2,000 years ago several springs of fresh water flowed down this hillside and into the Thames. It was the presence of these little streams which determined the positioning of this, the largest of the Roman bathhouses to be found. It goes without saying that a large bathhouse, rather like a modern Turkish bath, will need

14. How the Huggin Hill bathhouse would have looked when being built.

a plentiful supply of water and here was a limitless and abundant source. Illustration 14 shows what this bathhouse would have looked like when it was being built.

If we walk down the steps into the Cleary Garden, we reach a lower terrace. We are walking now through the remains of the cellars of buildings which stood on this site until they were destroyed by German bombs. Some of the brickwork which can be seen is very old, dating back to medieval times. This is still over a thousand years younger though than the wall at which we shall be looking. Carry on down to the grassy patch right at the bottom of the slope and then examine the wall on the left, which is partly obscured by vegetation. If you go to the very end of this wall, the farthest point down the hill that we can get without coming up against a fence, and then look at the lowest level, a wall of white blocks of limestone will be seen. This is a retaining wall of the Roman bathhouse. It runs beneath the roadway and this is the only section which can now be seen. There are more remains of the structure in the basement of one of the modern office blocks which stand nearby, but they are not generally accessible. Illustration 15 shows the wall.

We have looked already at some of the reasons why the Romans chose this part of the Thames Valley first for a military base and then later for the city which would become the capital of this province of the Empire. It is time to see another of the topographical features which made this such an ideal and defensible spot. Walk back to the entrance of the Cleary Garden and retrace your steps along Friday Street.

15. Retaining wall of the bathhouse, still visible.

When you reach the main road, turn left into Cannon Street and continue walking along the street until you find yourself standing in front of St Paul's Cathedral. Turning your back on the cathedral, look down the street ahead of you. This is Ludgate Hill and looking down it from this spot, you do get a sense of being on a hill.

Armies love hills, because if they establish a position on the top of a hill and it comes to a struggle between infantry, then those on the hill have an advantage. Anybody seeking to attack them and dislodge them from their stronghold will be obliged to charge uphill. So having found some higher, dry ground, as close as possible to the ford itself, on which to establish their base, the army saw at once that this would be a good strategic positions for that reason alone. The hill upon which we are now standing was part of a gravel terrace, covered with a layer of brickearth, which rose above the marshes and made a suitable location for tents to be pitched. We have already visited the other part of this little plateau, Cornhill.

The other good point about the twin hills of Cornhill and Ludgate is that they are surrounded on two sides by rivers. When we stood at the top of Huggin Hill earlier and looked down the hill, it was very obvious that we were looking at a slope down towards the river. The Thames was, as we have said, much wider 2,000 years ago than it is today. The water's edge would have been right at the very bottom of Huggin Hill, along the line of what are today Upper and Lower Thames Streets. This meant that any attacking force who had it in mind to seize Ludgate Hill from the south would have been obliged to swim across the Thames, which was at that point perhaps a mile and a half wide in those days, and then charge up a hill to engage the defenders. Not an enticing prospect.

Standing now at the top of Ludgate Hill, looking west, we can see that this too is definitely a hill, which leads down to where a busy road crosses it at the bottom. Two thousand years ago though, there would not have been any sort of road at the bottom of Ludgate Hill, busy or not. Instead, one would have found a river.

It is time to visit another of the rivers which at the time of which we are writing ran through central London. Walk down the slope of Ludgate Hill and you are approaching the western limit of the Roman city. On the right, you will come to a church called St Martin within Ludgate. The name of this church tells us that we are at the spot where there was a gate in the wall which encircled Londinium from the beginning of the third century. The church was built just within, or in other words inside, the city gate which once stood here. Indeed, in the crypt of this church, although not usually accessible to public view, is a section of Roman masonry from the old wall.

As you near the bottom of the hill, it is possible to see that Fleet Street, the road which is really a continuation of Ludgate Hill, slopes upwards. This is because we are entering a river valley, that of the Fleet. This was a good protection for the city, ensuring that attack from this direction would be unlikely. At the bottom of the hill, we pause at the main road, along which a never-ending stream of traffic thunders past at right-angles to the direction in which we are walking. Behind us, a little way up Ludgate Hill, stood one of the gates which led into the Roman city of Londinium. Before us would have lain a river which flowed into the Thames at what is now Blackfriars Bridge. There were two islands to our right, on which the Romans built a mill and, possibly, a temple. Looking up Farringdon Road to the right shows us clearly that we are standing in a river valley. We see in the distance what appears to be a bridge crossing the busy road. This is Holborn Viaduct, which was built in the nineteenth century because horse-drawn vehicles found it very taxing to go down the hill on one side of the old river and then up the other. The viaduct marks the location where Watling Street left the Roman city.

While here, we can visit another little-known remaining part of Roman London, this time a mosaic floor which may be seen *in situ*, just as it was laid almost 2,000 years ago. If we cross the road and head up Fleet Street, we are now on the other side of the river which ran along the west side of the Roman city and served to discourage attack from that direction. An alley way on the left leads us to a dark courtyard which contains one of Wren's most famous churches, that of St Bride's.

To understand the context of what we are about to see, it is necessary to know a little about Roman customs when it came to death and burial. Like many cultures, the Romans had taboos around the disposal of corpses. Burial was not generally allowed within a city, but cemeteries were established outside, along the roads leading to them. This served a dual purpose. It prevented living people from sharing their space with corpses or cremated remains and it also ensured that people would not fade from memory. Those entering or leaving a city would be obliged to pass through an area of monuments and tombs. The most highly sought-after spots for people to erect a tomb to their dead husbands, wives or children were those right next to the road, so that passers-by would be sure to see them and perhaps read the name on the tomb, thus keeping alive the memory of the dead person.

Outside the city of Londinium, there were cemeteries on the roads leading into the city. At Southwark, the streets of tombs were combined with a temple complex. Along the valley of the Fleet, where we now find ourselves, there were burials both in this area and further north, where Holborn Viaduct now stands. The area where we are now standing was used for burials when the Romans were in London; one such burial of a woman was unearthed within the crypt of the church itself.

Looking up at the spire of St Bride's reminds us at once of a layered wedding cake and this resemblance is not coincidental. The first traditional wedding cake of the kind familiar to us all was, according to legend, produced in the late eighteenth century by an apprentice baker called William Rich, who worked in premises on the other side of Fleet Street. The story is that he was casting around for inspiration for a spectacular cake and happened to see the spire of St Bride's while he was planning how to construct this marvel. The rest, as they say, is history. How much truth there is in this tale will be for readers to decide for themselves.

It is possible that the association of the church with weddings and fertility may not be coincidental. There was until the nineteenth century a well near to the church. Indeed, it may be that the well itself was the very reason that a church was founded on the spot. It was not uncommon to find a temple associated with a Roman burial ground. We have a similar arrangement today, when many churches are sited in the midst of graveyards. It is entirely possible that something of the kind was found here. There are two reasons for supposing this to be likely. The first is that the name of the church, St Bride's, is very unusual, and this is the only example of the use of that name in eastern Britain. 'Bride' is the Irish pronunciation of the name Bridget, who was an Irish saint living in the fifth and sixth centuries AD. It is thought though that Bridget was an attempt by Christians to appropriate the Celtic goddess Brigid, who was once worshipped in Britain and Ireland. Certainly, the well here was known as Bride's Well. Knowing the importance which was attached by the Celts to springs and wells, it is quite possible that this well had some supernatural significance. Although this is not perhaps the place to explore the matter in great detail, it is work recalling that the feast day of St Bride, also known as St Brigid, is 1 February. It is probably no coincidence that the Celtic festival of Imbolc also falls upon this day and is a time of renewal and fertility.

Entering the churchyard of St Bride's, we pause and consider a fact which was mentioned earlier, that the horrors of the Blitz brought to light many things which had been hidden from sight for centuries or even, as in the case of St Bride's, millennia. The church was gutted by a fire caused by the incendiaries which the Luftwaffe showered upon the city, and when the time came to rebuild, excavations revealed some astonishing discoveries buried deep within the foundations. These include the remains of earlier churches on the site, but most interesting to us was the uncovering of a Roman floor from a building which had stood on the site since the second century AD. Even before this floor had been laid, the Romans had been busy here digging a large trench, the purpose of which is quite unknown. It was some distance from the city and on the other side of the Fleet, so what they were about here is not at all clear.

Entering the church, we are able to descend a flight of stairs leading down to the very foundations and find that the church of St Bride's was built on the site of a Roman building of unknown purpose. If we enter the chapel and walk to the end of it, we are able to see two mirrors, set pointing downwards at an angle of 45 degrees and in which may be seen the plain mosaic floor which was discovered during the rebuilding of the church after the end of the war. This floor may be seen in Illustration 16. Nobody knows whether this floor formed part of an ordinary domestic structure, somebody's house, or whether it was a temple. There seems no good reason why anybody should have chosen to build a house so far from away from all the other buildings of Londinium, outside the city walls and on the other side of the river

16. Roman floor, visible at St Bride's Church.

from everybody else. Because there was an ancient well, regarded as being holy, on the site of the church, it has been suggested that the Roman remains are those of a very early temple, which later became a church, one of the earliest in Europe perhaps. The truth is, nobody knows for sure. All we can say is that here is a section of Roman floor which may be found just the way it was laid almost 2,000 years ago.

We have so far limited ourselves to what might called the main part of Roman London, the square mile of the modern-day City of London. From a very early time though, the Romans also occupied that part of the area which was found at the other end of the bridge which they built. This district is known today as Southwark and it also played an important role in the development of the city. In the next chapter, we shall cross the bridge and see what traces of Roman London are to be found across the river.

Chapter 4

Southwark

So far, we have explored only that part of Central London which lies north of the Thames. We now cross the river and see what was going on in Southwark, the district which faces the City of London on the south bank. For a long while, historians neglected this part of Roman London, assuming that not all that much happened 'across the water', as those who live north of the Thames sometimes snobbishly refer to south London. It is now known though that there must have been a fairly substantial settlement in Southwark very early on in the Roman occupation of Britain. This is because archaeologists have discovered that the so-called 'Red Layer', associated with Boudicca's burning of Londinium, is also to be found in Southwark. This suggests that there were buildings in that part of the city which were considered worth torching and that there were enough of them to generate the fierce heat which produced the layer of oxidized iron and burnt clay found on the other side of the river.

We begin our exploration of Southwark by taking the London Underground to Monument Station. On leaving the exit leading to Fish Street Hill, turn right after a few yards and walk down Fish Street Hill. This was the original path of the Roman road which led straight from the forum to the bridge. The Roman bridge was a few yards to the east of the modern London Bridge. After passing the Monument on your left, which commemorates the Great Fire of London in 1666, you will come to a busy road called Lower Thames Street. On the other side of this road, directly opposite where you are standing, can be seen the church of St Magnus the Martyr. Cross the road and walk into the porch of this church, an open space beneath the tower. There you will find a large wooden beam, the oldest relic of Roman London on public display anywhere in the city. It was part of the quay where ships unloaded when they arrived at Londinium. A plaque attached to this piece of timber says, 'FROM ROMAN WHARF A.D. 75 FOUND FISH STREET HILL 1931'. In fact, dendrochronological study of this wood reveals that it is older than that; it is from a tree felled in 62 AD, just a couple of years after the Boudiccan destruction of Londinium. More will be said on the subject of dendrochronology in a later chapter, for it was of great use in establishing the age and length of use of London's amphitheatre.

Fish Street Hill is of course the road along which we walked before crossing Lower Thames Street to reach the church and the fact that this piece of wood from the wharf was found there is another indication of how much wider the Thames was a couple of thousand years ago. All the land from Fish Street Hill to the present boundary of the river has been reclaimed.

It is time to cross the river and look at Roman Southwark. On leaving St Magnus the Martyr, turn left and walk along Lower Thames Street, passing beneath London Bridge. When you have done so, you will see that on the opposite side of the street is a flight of steps which will lead you up the bridge itself. Turn right at the top of the steps and you can make your way to Southwark.

For topographical reasons the main part of the city of Londinium was established on the north bank of the River Thames. However, a suburb sprang up on the south bank, centred around the crossing there. We do not know whether the first means of crossing the Thames at this point was a ferry or pontoon bridge. There had been Roman settlement in this area almost as early as that on Cornhill, but it was all on a smaller scale and constrained by the nature of the terrain around the southern end of the bridge. These first buildings had been destroyed during the Boudiccan revolt and all that we will be looking at dates from after that time. Only the famous 'Red Layer' remains of that first iteration of Roman Southwark.

The important thing to remember when we explore Southwark is that it bore not the slightest resemblance to the district as we now know it. When the Romans arrived, Southwark consisted of a series of islands, separated at low tide by mudflats with streams flowing through them. At high tide, the whole area was submerged, apart from a few of the largest islands, on which the Romans built. The nature of the terrain in this part of the river placed a limit upon the development possible. Illustration 17 shows roughly how Southwark would have been at that time, a network of disconnected islands.

When you are nearly across the river, stop for a moment and look back across the Thames to the city. To your left, is the unmistakable sight of the dome of St Paul's Cathedral. To the right of it are the twin towers of Cannon Street Station, where the governor's palace very likely stood. Just to the left of the station is the outfall of the long-vanished Walbrook stream. Now look along London Bridge itself. The Roman bridge would have been a little to the east of the present one, that is to say a few yards to the right. Remember though that it would have been a good deal longer than the current bridge, because the Thames was

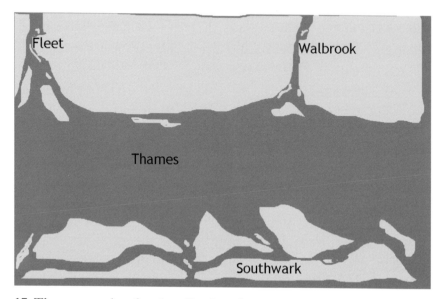

17. The topography of ancient Southwark.

much wider at that time. A little to the right of the bridge, you will see a church spire, that of St Magnus the Martyr. This is where we saw the piece of timber from the Roman wharfs which lay alongside the bridge and it is also very likely where the Roman bridge ended.

It is time to see what remains of the Roman city in Southwark. If you carry on walking in the direction in which you have been travelling, then you will come to a steep flight of stairs on your right. Making your way down these will bring you to a cobbled lane. It is surprising how many streets in this part of London are still cobbled, rather than being covered in asphalt. Turn right and walk along a little. To your left, you will see the towering bulk of Southwark Cathedral, which is our first destination. Everybody is familiar with London's other Anglican cathedral, St Paul's, but surprisingly few people have heard of this cathedral or are even aware that there is more than one cathedral in London. Southwark Cathedral, or the Cathedral and Collegiate Church of St Saviour and St Mary Overie, to give it its full name, was founded in the twelfth century, although there was already some kind of monastic order here and it is said that nuns lived here as early as the seventh century AD. This is curious, because it touches upon an idea which has already been mentioned, that of the persistence of memory which preserves concepts or ideas from Roman London which cling to certain locations and may be seen in their uses across the centuries and millennia. We saw such a thing with the London Stone and also when visiting St Bride's Church in Fleet Street. With this cathedral, it seems possible that there was a Roman temple or place of worship on this spot and that is why it mutated into a Christian church.

The history of the cathedral is interesting, but hardly germane to our exploration of the ancient Roman city! Turn left and walk across an open space to the entrance to the cathedral. Once inside, turn left again and you will find what is described as the 'archaeological chamber'. This allows us to gaze back through the centuries and millennia. Part of the original Saxon foundations of the church can be

18. The Roman road beneath Southwark Cathedral.

glimpsed, as well as a seventeenth-century kiln. These are interesting, but the most remarkable sight of all is part of the original Roman road which led to the bridge across the Thames. This is the only place in London where it is possible to see a Roman road *in situ*. This section of metalled road may be seen in Illustration 18.

This road is Watling Street, which led from Dover to London. Another Roman road, Stane Street, joined it somewhere in the region of what is now Borough High Street. This is the road which would have carried traffic across the bridge and into the main part of Londinium, which we explored in the last chapter.

Turning to your right, you will see a glass case which contains a replica of the statue of a god. This is a hunter, who wears a Phrygian cap which puts one in mind of Mithras, but this man is in a particular pose and accompanied by two cult animals more appropriate to Apollo or Diana. The dog and deer at his side hint that this is a hunter. There are distinct similarities between this figure and the one carved onto the altar found beneath Goldsmiths' Hall, at which we will look in Chapter 7. It may be that this is a peculiarly British deity, with no precise equivalent among the pantheon of gods worshipped by the Romans. The discovery of this enigmatic sculpture might perhaps cast light upon the origins of the cathedral itself as a place of Christian worship. Illustration 19 shows this strange figure.

In 1977, it was decided to open a sealed burial vault which lay beneath the choir stalls. This crypt had been constructed in 1703 and sealed in the 1840s. When it was entered, many old coffins were of course discovered and they were removed for reburial elsewhere.

19. Hunter god, found buried under Southwark Cathedral.

Once this had been done, it was found that those excavating the vault had dug down to the ground level of the late first century. A well was found, dating from that time and clogged with broken masonry. It is curious to see the presence of a well beneath a church in this way. It will be recalled that a well also existed on the site of St Bride's on the other side of the river. There is an old tradition in Britain of holy wells. The presence of wells beneath Christian churches might be a sign that they were erected here in order to appropriate a pagan place of worship. This well was skilfully made, with timber holding apart the walls of the shaft.

The objects found hidden in the well certainly reinforced the idea that there was an earlier place of worship here, dating back to the Roman occupation. That this had been a place of importance to the Romans in the centuries following the occupation of Britain was obvious, because an altar, a tombstone and the image of a pagan god, together with other broken miniature statues of deities, were all found deep within the well. These were broken and blackened, as though attempts had been made to damage or destroy them. The early Christians were notoriously intolerant of any other religions and it has been suggested that these items had been damaged when Christians sacked a Roman temple which at one time stood on this site. Perhaps worshippers of the old gods retrieved them and then cast them down the well to save them from further harm. We might at this point anticipate what will be said in the later chapter about religion in Roman London. For some reason, horned animals and gods seemed to play an enormously significant part in religious practice in Londinium and this is especially notable where we are now, which is to say south of the Thames. Perhaps a few examples will make this clearer.

The hunter god which was found beneath Southwark Cathedral has similarities with statues of Diana, who was for the Romans the goddess of hunting. He carries a bow and arrows, which were Diana's usual weapons, and has at his side both a dog and a stag. It was with the hunting of the stag which Diana was most associated. In Britain, since the end of the Ice Age the stag has been the largest wild animal to be found. Stags are of course distinguished by their antlers. This then is one religious connection with horned beasts from south London at the time that the Romans occupied the area. A few hundred yards from here was a Romano-Celtic temple complex, which will be described in detail in the chapter on religion. For now though, two discoveries made there shed light upon the idea that horned beasts and men with antlers or horns were popular in Roman London in a religious context. The first of these was the finding of a bronze cloven hoof from a statue of Pan, the god of wild places. He was half human and half goat, noted for the horns upon his head. Of even more significance was a marble plaque which detailed how a wealthy patron had paid for renovations of the temples. It read as follows, 'To the Divinities of the Emperors and to the god Mars Camulus, Tiberius Celaranius, a citizen of the Bellovaci, morotix, of Londoners'. This is the first known use of the word 'Londoners', but of more interest now is the fact that it is a dedication to Mars Camulus. This is one of those composite gods, partly Roman and partly based upon a Celtic divinity. Mars Camulus is known from other inscriptions and is always shown with horns upon his head.

We shall be visiting the site of a Romano-Celtic temple in Greenwich in a later chapter. Found there was part of a statue of a female. This looked very much as though it was from a statue of Diana, the goddess of hunting, for it represented a hand reaching back to pluck an arrow from a quiver.

Many gods and goddesses were worshipped or honoured in Roman London and it does seem that there was some preference for those connected in some way with horned animals or even mythological figures who were partly human and bore horns on their heads. When we visit the Temple of Mithras on the other side of the river, we shall see this same theme emerging, for the central figure of Mithraism, featured on every altar, was a bull being slain by Mithras. Yet another horned animal.

It is certain that a Roman building of some kind stood on this spot before the Saxons built their church here. If you go into the main body of the church, you will find a section of Roman flooring, the reddish-brown tesserae which we have seen associated with other ancient churches in London such as St Brides and All Hallows by the Tower. Some have suggested that a villa stood here, but there is the possibility that it was a temple. Without further evidence, we are unlikely ever to know for sure.

If you leave Southwark Cathedral by the same door by which you entered it and then walk to the street, we can visit one of the most important Roman sites in this part of London. Turn left, once you are in the street, and then follow the road round to the right, hugging the buildings on your right until you reach a dock which contains a sailing ship. This is a replica of Sir Francis Drake's ship, the *Golden Hinde*. Opposite this ship, on the left, is a pedestrian street which will lead you to one of the most remarkable and little-known old buildings in the whole of London.

Towering above you as you walk between the tall buildings which rise on either side of this narrow street is the remains of a huge medieval hall. High up on the end of one wall is an enormous rose window. This is shown in Illustration 20. This was once one of the most important buildings in London. It is the Bishop of Winchester's Palace and for centuries it simply disappeared from view. Its survival is little short of a miracle. Founded in the twelfth century, the palace remained in use for 500 years, until in the seventeenth century it was divided up into tenements and warehouses. Other buildings were erected around the palace, until it was completely hidden from view. As the years passed, its very existence was forgotten. A fire during Queen Victoria's reign caused some of the later walls and other additions to collapse, revealing for the first time in centuries the rose window of the original palace. In the 1980s, work was done on the ruins of the palace to spruce them up a little and the result may be seen today.

20. Winchester Palace in Southwark.

I dare say that readers are scratching their heads at this point and asking themselves what this medieval palace has to do with Roman London. The answer is that this is yet another instance of what has been described as the persistence of memory in the streets of London. A thousand years before the Bishop of Winchester caused a palace to be built on this spot, there already existed a palace, which had been constructed by the Romans; for what purpose, we do not know.

We have already looked at the possible site of the governor's residence, which now lies beneath Cannon Street Station. Where you are now standing though, another grand building was situated and it was so large and finely decorated that the suggestion has even been mooted that far from being on the other side of the river, the palace of the Roman governor actually stood here, in Southwark. Let us look at the evidence and see what grounds there might be for believing this.

Between 1983 and 1990, a lot of building and redevelopment was carried out in and around Winchester Palace. This gave archaeologists from the Museum of London a perfect opportunity to explore the area and what they found astonished them. One discovery was a bathhouse with an area of perhaps 650m2. This consisted of a suite of seven rooms, which was about the size of the public bathhouse at Huggin Hill which was mentioned in the last chapter. Inscriptions found suggest that the bathhouse in Southwark might have been intended purely for military use, which given the size would indicate the presence of a large garrison in the area. A bathhouse was found in Cheapside, on the other side of the river, and its proximity to the fort which stood nearby caused some researchers to think that this too was intended solely for military use. The one in Southwark though was about twice the size of that in Cheapside. If that one catered for the thousand or so soldiers who were stationed at the fort, then it might be that the one found near Winchester Palace served even more than that. Another possibility of course is that it was large and luxurious because it was set up not for ordinary infantrymen, but rather for senior officers.

Not only a bathhouse stood here. There was a fine building, decorated with the most complete wall paintings which have ever been found in London. We may see one of these in Illustration 21. It would not look out of place in a villa at Pompeii. This was no villa though; it had something to do with the governance of London, although just what that means is still a mystery. There are clues, however.

The first clue is the discovery of tiles stamped 'CLBR'. This is of great interest, because almost all the previous examples of tiles marked in this way have come from Dover. The reason for this is very simple. 'CLBR' stands for '*Classis Britannica*', the British fleet. Such tiles have only been found south of London and east of Beachy Head

21. Wall painting from Roman building in Southwark.

in Sussex, with most found at Dover. They have also turned up in the French port of Boulogne. Their presence in Southwark indicates certainly that the buildings excavated here were official, rather than domestic, but combined with an inscription which was also unearthed, they lead to the conclusion that the buildings here were in some way part of a military complex. The question is of course, what kind of military complex and how important was it?

The inscription found was fragmentary and appeared to list military units by cohort. This has been interpreted as relating to some guild of officers, perhaps centurions. Combined with the tiles, at the very least it seems probable that on the site where Winchester Palace was later built there was once an important and grand building which had some connection with the Roman armed forces. That much can probably be asserted without fear of contradiction. Some people though, have gone a good deal further than this in speculating about the precise nature of the building.

One theory is that the headquarters of the Roman fleet in Britain was here in Southwark. Considering the importance of Londinium and the fact that it was a large port, this idea is by no means implausible. There was certainly plenty of room for the fleet to operate out of London and having the naval headquarters in the city would have made sense. An even more daring idea is that this was actually the governor's palace and that the site which now lies beneath Cannon Street Station is no more than a public bathhouse or something of that kind. This would elevate Southwark to the position of administrative centre for the entire province. Although this idea has its advocates, there is little general enthusiasm for it. A variation, which is perhaps more possible, is that the head of the civil administration was, as has long been thought, in the region of Cannon Street, but that the centre of military power was found here in Southwark.

What does seem beyond a doubt is that 40 years ago, Roman Southwark was widely viewed as a relatively recent and insignificant part of the city of Londinium. Even the discovery that Boudicca and her army had bothered to sack and burn Southwark came as a surprise when it came to light a few years ago. Today, it is acknowledged that the city south of the river was an integral and important part of Londinium. It is interesting to ask ourselves if this neglect of archaeological research in Londinium south of the Thames, together with the opinion that nothing much of importance happened there, might be part of the traditional and dismissive way that those living north of the river have been accustomed to talk of, and view, south London. Even today, those who live north of that Thames are in the habit of referring to south London as 'Across the water' and joking that it is like a foreign country there.

It is by no means impossible that readers will by this time be heartily sick and tired of hearing that they must now 'retrace their steps'! There is, unfortunately, no other way of moving about through some of the older parts of London and this is one of those cases. This time, retracing our steps will bring us back to the stairs which we came down to reach Southwark Cathedral. If we now ascend those same steps, we will find ourselves once more on London Bridge. Turning right and then crossing the road will take us to London Bridge Station. We need to head not towards the Tube station, but rather for the main entrance of the railway station itself. Once there, we will find that that great symbol of modernity, the office building known as the 'Shard', looms above us. We need to walk past this, so that it is on our left, and then travel down an escalator which will take us to a street straight ahead of us and called Great Maze Pond. This is a curious name for a street, and we shall see shortly why it was so called.

If we walk along Great Maze Pond, we will be passing through Guy's Hospital, the various buildings of which are scattered all over this part of Southwark. Eventually, we come on our left to a fairly new building, which is the cancer centre. By now, we have walked some considerable distance from the Thames, and it may come as something of a surprise to learn that buried and preserved beneath the building in front of us is a complete Roman boat. What could a boat possibly have been doing so far from the river? The answer is of course that this was not at all far from the river and that the place where we are now standing was, at the time of Roman London, open water.

Roman Southwark was established upon two islands. The whole of this part of south London was a mixture of marshes, mudflats, rivers and islands. Although the Romans did their best to reclaim land from the river, the situation persisted in parts of this area until the Victorian era. The reason that this street is called Great Maze Pond is that there really were ponds here and people driving cattle to market in central London used to water their herds around here. These ponds were the remnants of a creek upon which Guy's Hospital is now built. The Roman boat was simply plying the waterways in this part of London when it became unseaworthy and was abandoned in the mudflats. When the nearby cancer centre was built, the boat was examined and found to be in good condition and left where it was.

Those rivers are still around, although like the Fleet and Walbrook, they now flow underground. It is possible to see one of them though. If readers wish to go back to London Bridge Station and then down to Tooley Street, which runs east and parallel to the River Thames, they will come, in something over half a mile, to a turning on the left called Shad Thames. Walking down this, they will come, on their right, to a river which is flowing into the Thames at this point. Crossing the footbridge over this, it can be seen that this river actually extends for some way into the streets of south London. This is the Neckinger and it cut off part of this area, which formed an island in the nineteenth century. This was known as Jacob's Island and it was a notorious slum district. Bill Sikes had his home here in Dickens' *Oliver Twist*. It is rivers like this which once crisscrossed the marshy area of Southwark.

The whole of Southwark was once like this, islands surrounded by mudflats and marshes. At high tide, the water of the Thames would lap up to the very edge of these islands, but even at low tide they would be surrounded by mud, through which streams of water ran. It is hard to imagine Roman Southwark when we are walking the streets of the modern district, because of course all the waterways and rivers have been forced underground. We saw this, of course, on the other side of the Thames, when we traced the line of the Walbrook and Fleet. There at least, there are still some faint indications of the slopes and depressions which show where once there was a valley. In Southwark, nothing of the kind remains and the land is now completely flat. It is only in the street names, such as Great Maze Pond, that we see any hint of water. The Romans began this process, and it was continued over the centuries, until today we are mystified to be told that a Roman boat should be buried beneath the foundations of some building in the area.

From Great Maze Pond, we carry on walking in the same direction, crossing the road and then continuing along a street called Crosby Row. This brings us to a very modern development where extensive archaeological work was conducted before the buildings went up. It was already known that this was the site both of a cemetery and also a temple, but the excavation revealed far more than had previously been known about the area when it straddled the road leading to Londinium. To begin with there were at least two Romano-Celtic temples here, set about 130ft apart. They shared an altar, which was set up in an open space between them. As was usual with such temples at that time, each consisted of an open area where worshippers would gather and also a building which was accessible only to the priests. At Tabard Square, the area where we are now standing, the courtyards were fringed with stone pillars which supported a covered walkway, rather like the cloisters of a medieval monastery. The open area for the common people was called the *temenos* and the structure of the temple itself was the *cella*. These indicated graduations of sacred space. The *temenos* was sacred, but the *cella* was, if you like, the holy of holies.

Mention was made earlier of a marble plaque which was found near here, dedicated to Mars Camulus. A commemorative stone bearing the inscription in Latin and English may be found here in Tabard Square. More will be said about the temples which once stood here in another chapter.

In this and the two preceding chapters, we have covered by foot the area which is traditionally thought to comprise the city of Londinium. Now we turn our attention to somewhere which is not usually associated with the Romans in London; a district a mile and a half from the city walls. In doing so, we must bear in mind that controversy surrounds this subject, and that archaeologists and historians fiercely debate whether or not the title of the next chapter, mentioning as it does 'Roman Westminster', even has any meaning.

Chapter 5

The Mystery of Roman Westminster

For the last thousand years or so, London has been a city of two halves. The old area which was the one enclosed by the wall built by the Romans, the so-called Square Mile, is the centre of finance and trading. Refer to 'the City', and this is immediately understood. To the west is where political power is based. 'Westminster' is shorthand meaning the government and legislature. The City of London and Westminster were for a long while physically separate entities and it was only as they both gradually expanded that the two eventually merged into one urban area, although divided by the perception of citizens into two distinct realms; the mercantile and the political. It is traditionally assumed that this situation originated with Edward the Confessor, the pious king who caused a monastery to be founded where Westminster Abbey now stands and also had a royal palace built nearby.

By this reading of history, the area where Westminster Abbey is now was deserted fenland when Edward the Confessor took it into his head that there should be a monastery dedicated to St Peter where the old ford across the Thames was located. Although there had been a Saxon settlement around the area of Covent Garden and the Strand, this did not extend as far as Westminster Abbey.

There is a slight problem with this idea and in recent years more and more evidence has emerged which indicates that something was happening around what is now Westminster as long ago as the first century AD, soon after the arrival of the Romans in Britain. There is a good deal of controversy about this idea, but it is only fair to include some account of it in a book which is devoted to the exploration of Roman London.

At the end of Chapter 2, we looked at the church of St Bride's in Fleet Street and saw what remains of a Roman building which once stood where the church is now. A Roman burial was uncovered at the same time as the floor of the building and it has been claimed that this was undertaken according to Christian rites, which in turn means that there was a church on the site from the fourth or fifth century AD. Other burials, chiefly of cremated remains in pots and vases, have also been found in the area, most notably at the junction of Shoe Lane and Fleet Street, only a stone's throw from St Bride's.

The explanation for these burials is supposedly that because of the proximity of the River Fleet to the city gate which was on Ludgate Hill, the traditional cemetery which might reasonably have been expected to be found just outside the gate, as at Aldgate and Bishopsgate, was instead established on the other side of the river. This is plausible and provides a good and sufficient explanation for the burials found in the area around St Bride's. What is curious though is that burials are found a lot further west of the city wall than that. Indeed, during building work at Westminster Abbey itself in the nineteenth century, a large Roman sarcophagus was found. In 1869, this massive stone coffin was uncovered. It bore an inscription which has been dated stylistically to the third or fourth century AD and read as follows, 'Memoriae Valeri Amandini Valeri Superventor et (Valerius) Marcellus patri fecer(unt)'. This translates as 'To the memory of Valerius Amandinus; Valerius Superventor and Valerius Marcellus made this for their father'. This sarcophagus is on display in Westminster Abbey, in the newly-opened roof space, or triforium, there.

On the face of it, discovering a very heavy stone coffin like this is a bit of a puzzle. Was it carried all the way from Ludgate, simply to be buried miles away in what was practically a swamp? The lid though gives us a clue that all might not be as it at first seems, because it is carved with a cross, which was almost certainly done a long time after the sarcophagus itself was made. It had been suggested that this was a case of Saxons reusing a Roman artifact which they had come across nearer to the city and then bringing it, perhaps by water, to this spot to be buried.

The thing is though, that this is not an isolated incident of such a discovery, and it is not only Roman burials which have been found this far from the walls of Londinium. In fact, such burials are scattered all the way along Fleet Street and the Strand, as far as Trafalgar Square. Now this is odd, if we assume that they are all of them connected in some way with a supposed cemetery outside the city walls near Ludgate. In the other such cemeteries at Southwark, Aldgate and Bishopsgate, the burials are tightly clustered together. This makes perfect sense. If you are going to conduct a funeral, you don't want to be lugging some great stone coffin, literally weighing a ton, for miles. Rather, you will be inclined to have the grave as close to where you live as possible, so that you will be able to visit it if the mood should take you.

When the present church of St Martin-in-the-Fields was being built in the early eighteenth century, two massive stone sarcophagi was found. Both were Roman. It really does stretch credulity beyond breaking point that a funeral procession would emerge from the city at Ludgate and then transport such things a mile and a half along the road to bury them in the deserted field which Trafalgar Square supposedly was at that time. Far more likely is that they were interred near to where the family actually lived. But did the Roman city extend as far as Westminster? Were people actually living around this part of London at that time? Discoveries made beneath the church of St Martin-in-the-Fields between 2005 and 2007 threw up some amazing finds.

The clergy at St Martin-in-the-Fields were delighted when archaeologists from the Museum of London found a stone sarcophagus weighing a ton and a half during their dig, for it allowed them to claim this as evidence that the church might have been established on this spot in Roman times, which would make it the earliest church in London. Nicholas Holtam, the vicar, announced that, 'This find is extraordinarily moving. It raises the possibility that this has been a sacred site for much longer than we previously thought. The sarcophagus and body are from the time of St Martin himself, who died in 397 AD.' There could be little doubt about the date of the burial, nor that it was Roman, because nearby, a coin from the reign of Constantius (355–65 AD) was discovered. This was interesting, but by no means the most exciting thing to be revealed during the excavations.

Evidence was found of several wooden buildings, which dated from the first to the third centuries AD. These indicated that there was a permanent presence in this part of London from the very first years of the Roman occupation, but the most surprising find was a kiln, which had been built to produce the typical Roman tiles of the kind which we saw in Illustration 11 (see page 27). Such a structure would hardly have been erected in this area had there not been buildings which required tiles for their roofs. It was the date which was so surprising. By means of archaeomagnetic dating, it was found that the last time the kiln had been fired was between 400 and 500 AD. This made it remarkable for a number of reasons. First, of course, this was the first Roman kiln to have been discovered in central London. One was excavated some years ago in Highgate, but never so close to the area of Londinium itself. The second point of interest was that this kiln was the most recent structure ever found in London from the Roman period. Finally, the date of the last use of the kiln suggested that work was still being carried out and either new roofs being made, or old ones repaired, at a time when historians generally assume that Roman London was falling into ruin and decay. Regardless of what might be taking place in the walled city itself, Roman workmen in this area were still hard at work, producing building materials in the traditional style.

The work in and around St Martin-in-the-Fields confirmed what many had suspected, that far from being the neat and compact little city, enclosed and defined by that famous wall, that we have always supposed, Londinium was actually larger and more interesting. Traces of other Roman buildings have been regularly found west of the City of

London and it was probably the case that a straggling line of buildings stretched along what is now Fleet Street, through the Strand and at least as far as Trafalgar Square and Westminster Abbey. How else to account for what was unearthed beneath the abbey itself in 1878, when digging the grave of Sir Gilbert Scott? There, right in the middle of the nave, was found part of a hypocaust, which suggested that a fairly grand building had stood on this site a thousand years before Edward the Confessor chose this spot for his monastery and palace. Nor was this all. While digging the foundations of new canons' houses in the Abbey garden a few years later, in 1883, remains of a Roman house were found. There was a concrete foundation and many roof tiles. This was a solid and well-built piece of work.

It is probably fair to say that Londinium did not stretch as far as Westminster, but of course as late as the medieval period this was still true, with the City of London and Westminster being two distinct entities, separated by a sparsely-populated ribbon of land which stretched along the north bank of the Thames. There is still an official acknowledgement that the City and Westminster are different polities. There is a point in Fleet Street where the Temple Bar once stood which marks the border between the two. It has been suggested that something of a similar state of affairs existed during the Roman occupation and that there was a settlement centred around where the Houses of Parliament and Westminster Abbey now stand, which was loosely connected with the main city of Londinium a few miles away. That a kiln was built and was turning out tiles at the time that the walled city of Londinium was falling into ruin is curious and might possibly suggest that Roman practices and the maintenance of some sort of Roman civilization lingered on for longer in Westminster than they did in what is now the City of London.

The discovery of the kiln beneath St Martin-in-the-Fields kickstarted the old controversy about the idea of Roman Westminster as an entity and it is likely that in the coming years, more research will take place which will shed further light upon this subject.

Chapter 6

London's Roman Roads

We have looked at several instances where the pattern of Roman London has noticeably affected the structure of the modern city. Nowhere is this tendency more obvious than in the street plan of London. Glancing at a map of London today enables us to see the skeleton of the city and its surroundings as they were 2,000 years ago and more. I say more, because of course when the Romans invaded Britain in 43 AD, they did not find an entirely blank canvas upon which they imposed their own civic planning. The geographical features of the land already existed and those living there had charted their own paths from one point to another and these included such things as the most convenient places to ford rivers and paths which had been made to avoid marshy land.

Let us begin by looking at a map of the old routes out of central London, before we surrounded the capital with ring roads, bypasses and all the other paraphernalia of town planning which we associate with the motor car. Starting in Bishopsgate, the road which runs from one of the gates leading out of Londinium when once there was a wall around the city, we can trace the route, which runs north, as straight as an arrow. It changes from Bishopsgate to Shoreditch High Street, and then into Kingsland Road. From there, the road becomes Stoke Newington High Street and then Stamford Hill, before becoming Tottenham High Road. This is of course the old Roman road which led to Cambridge, and its route is as clearly delineated today as it was when the legions first marched along it. Often, those living in London are vaguely aware of these straight main roads which run through the districts where they live, without stopping to ask themselves why it should be that one long road runs for many miles, without any interruption or change of direction. It seldom occurs to Londoners that these are perfect illustrations of the traditional idea of the Roman road, which marches over hill and dale without deviating from its path.

The road which we have looked at above is still sometimes called the Great North Road and it was for many years known as Ermine Street. This was not the Roman name for the road; it was called so by the Saxons. The major Roman routes across Britain often have names like this, which were given to them by Saxons and Vikings. We do not know if the Romans had any particular names for them.

Another example of such a road is that which led out of Londinium from the gate which became known in medieval times as Aldgate. It begins as Whitechapel Road, then becomes Mile End Road, and continues through Stratford, Forest Gate, Ilford and Seven Kings, running on in a straight line to Romford, which was a Roman settlement called Durolitum. This is of course the old Colchester Road, which took the Romans by the most direct way from London to the important city of Colchester, which was in the early years of the occupation the capital of the province. It was known in later years as the Great Road.

These are just two instances of the way in which the Roman roads have shaped London and its suburbs. The districts of Ilford and Seven Kings were deliberately developed as commuter towns in the early years of the twentieth century because they both lay on this route. The old roads have acted as London's arteries, shaping and helping to define the city which we see today.

Although London was not a city before the arrival of the Romans, tracks certainly passed through it and were regularly used by travellers. We remember that there was a good deal of trade and family connections between the Celts in what are now Belgium and France, and the Britons. These Celtic tribes had a common language and the headquarters of the druids, who were the holy men and priests of both Britain and Gaul, was on an island off the Welsh coast. Those sailing to and from Britain used the region which in which the city of Dover was later established, that part of the coast being a convenient point of arrival and departure. Once they landed here, they often wished to travel to what is now Colchester or even further afield to the druids' base on the Isle of Anglesey. This route, from Dover to north Wales, was the origin of the Roman road which became known to the Saxons as Watling Street. The course of this road has had a great influence on the modern city of London.

Before the Romans began to use Watling Street and turned it into a proper metalled road, it was really just a bridlepath, running in the first instance from Dover to London. Like other such paths, it may well have been marked with small monoliths on high ground, so that travellers could take bearings and be sure that they were not veering off in the wrong direction. As it approached London, the path passed through what is now Greenwich Park and then, almost without a shadow of a doubt, to the south bank of the Thames, opposite the location of the Houses of Parliament.

To anticipate something which will be discussed more fully in its proper context, Watling Street may well have been marked with small standing stones to guide those moving along it, but there were other landmarks too, which would have been visible for miles. Just as the Romans liked to bury their dead along the roadside, so too did the ancient Britons, and in some places, especially in southern Britain, they did this by digging deep ditches and then piling the spoil over the site of a burial. These are known as round barrows, and a field of such in central London may be seen in Illustration 22. In areas such as Greenwich, where these specimens may be found, the land is composed largely of chalk and when these great barrows, shaped like flying saucers, were set up on a hilltop, they would have been gleaming white. This would have acted almost like a beacon for travellers, telling them that they were still on the right track, so to speak.

Westminster was the first point of the Thames at which the river could be forded. There were various reasons for this, such as the fact

22. The ritual landscape of Greenwich; burial mounds.

that three tributaries converged nearby and there is a sharp bend in the course of the Thames as well. There is another good reason for thinking that there was a ford here and that is that the direction which the northern section of Watling Street points. The road runs all the way from the Shropshire town of Wroxeter to London. Londoners are familiar with the very southern end of the road, for it forms the Edgeware Road, which terminates at Marble Arch. Obviously, before Hyde Park and the Marble Arch itself blocked the way, the route south from the end of Edgeware Road continued to the Thames. A glance at the map shows us that this would have led straight to Westminster, the site of the supposed ford which was mentioned earlier.

Watling Street changed its course once the Romans had chosen the area around Cornhill and Ludgate Hill for their city. When they upgraded the Watling Street track and turned it into a proper road in the Roman style, it was brought from Greenwich to Southwark, where it crossed the bridge and then re-emerged from Londinium at Newgate. From there, it followed the line of High Holborn and Oxford Street, until it reached what is now Marble Arch. At this point, the road simply joined up with the old Watling Street and headed north. It is curious to reflect that Oxford Street is actually a remnant of the Roman road to the north of England. Like Ermine Street and the Great North Road through Tottenham, Watling Street carves its way in a straight line from central London, through the suburbs and then on into open country. Edgeware Road becomes Maida Vale, which turns into Kilburn High Street and Cricklewood, before heading up towards Hendon and then St Albans.

Just as the old roads have left their mark on the outer parts of the capital, so too is this the case in central London. One of the gates of the Roman city was near the junction of Newgate Street and Old Bailey, close to where the Central Criminal Court now stands. There is no longer any trace of the gateway, although a section of the wall remains in the basement of the court and can be seen during guided tours there. The streets here though follow precisely the same line that they did when the Romans were using them. Holborn Viaduct is on the site of the bridge which carried Watling Street over the River Fleet as it left the city and headed towards Marble Arch. Excavations at an office block next to the viaduct itself unearthed the cemetery which stood here at that time. We know that the roads which led in and out of Londinium were lined with tombs and this provides further confirmation that this was where the road to the north of England passed.

We are also able to trace the route of Watling Street a little way after it entered the city at Newgate. Newgate Street and Cheapside both lie precisely on the Roman street which was once here. On the other side of the City of London, Cannon Street and Eastcheap also coincide exactly with one of the main streets of Londinium, one which ran past what we assume to have been the palace of the governor, now buried beneath Cannon Street railway station. Running south from Eastcheap is Fish Street Hill, which also lies right above a Roman street, this time the one which led to the bridge which crossed the river at that point, a few yards downstream from today's London Bridge. It will be recalled that a piece of timber dating back to a year or two after the Boudiccan destruction of the city stands in the courtyard of the church of St Magnus the Martyr. This was either part of the bridge in 62 AD or possibly it was connected with the docks.

The structure of Roman London may be traced in modern streets in another way, by following the pattern imposed upon the city by the wall which encircled it for many centuries. The original Roman wall dictated the limit of London for many years and was added to throughout the medieval period. We can see the shape of the Roman city by simply following a few streets.

Aldgate is the site of the gate in the city wall from which the so-called Great Road led east and then north to Colchester. If we stand at that point in Aldgate High Street where the road called Minories joins it, then we are at the very point where the Roman road left Londinium. If we cross the road from this point and head north-west along Duke's Place, which faces Minories, then we shall be walking along a line which marks the interior of the city wall, which would have been on our right. We shall be exploring this route in detail in a later chapter, but for now we consider that Duke's Place turns firstly into Bevis Marks and then Camomile Street, until it reaches Bishopsgate, the site, as its name suggests, of another of the gates in the old city wall. Running parallel with us on the right of Bevis Marks is a street called Houndsditch, which is built upon the site of the moat or ditch which once lay as a defensive measure just beyond the city wall. Crossing Bishopsgate and continuing in the same direction will take us along Wormwood Street, which then becomes a road called London Wall, which is certainly a clear-enough clue as to its origin. Walking along London Wall as far as Moorgate will also mean that we are tracing the line of the city wall. The very bones of the Roman city are therefore clearly visible, if you know where to look.

Another instance of the modern streets in the City of London showing clearly where the limits of Londinium lay thousands of years ago may be seen by going to the Central Criminal Court, which may be found at the junction of Newgate Street and Old Bailey. The name of the street is of course now used more commonly, and incorrectly, to describe the Central Criminal Court. If one reads of a case being heard at the Old Bailey, we know at once that this refers to the court rather than the street. The name of Newgate Street, as with Aldgate and Bishopsgate, tells us that we are at the point where another gate led from the Roman city. In this instance, this is where Watling Street led west towards the region of Marble Arch.

Walking south along Old Bailey will entail our following once again the line of the city wall. It would have been on our left. When we reach Ludgate Hill, another gate would have been in the middle of the road to our left. Ludgate Hill itself runs precisely along the line of the Roman road which once ran to the gate here and from there across the river which lay at the bottom of the hill. Fleet Street, which is in a sense no more than a continuation of Ludgate Hill, shows where the Roman road ran after it left Londinium and headed west.

We saw a small section of a Roman road which is still visible today in Southwark Cathedral. This is, unfortunately, the only actual part of a Roman road which we can still see in London. One section of the city wall, at which we shall be looking, has a gravel pathway still intact, which runs parallel with the wall, but it would be stretching it a little to describe this as a road. It is time now to look at part of Roman London which is on open display, but is passed every day by people who do not even realize what it is. This is London's fort, which is a good deal larger than the better-known ones at Hadrian's Wall.

Chapter 7

London's Fort

For years, various academics had argued for the likelihood that there had once been a Roman fort in the capital, but nobody quite seemed to know where it might have been. Just as with some other Roman sites at which we shall look, it was the Blitz which brought the fort to light and enabled us to see parts of it. Drawing attention to the fort and proving where it had been and where its remains were now to be found was largely the work of one man, about whom we shall learn more shortly.

Most readers probably have at least a vague idea about the nature of Roman forts. The one at Housesteads, on Hadrian's Wall, is perhaps the most famous in Britain. London's own fort was much larger than those on the Scottish border, about three times the area. This makes it all the more surprising that it should have been concealed for so long. Two things caused it to emerge and be seen for what it was. One was the dogged persistence of W.F. Grimes, the archaeologist in charge of the Museum of London in the years following the end of the Second World War, and the other was the damage wrought by the German bombing to some of the old buildings in central London, which laid bare their cellars and the foundations upon which they had been built.

In Chapter 2 we looked at the early history of Londinium and saw that it had been destroyed in the Boudiccan revolt 10 or 12 years after it had been founded. Nothing was left of that first incarnation of London other than a layer of charred wood and burnt clay. It was not in the nature of the Roman occupiers to let a reverse like this deter them, however. That was not how a mighty empire had been forged. Within a year of the total destruction of the city, a fort had been built on the hill where the first settlement had been established, the area we know today as Cornhill. Remains of this first fort have been uncovered and dated to 63 AD. This was a fairly makeshift affair of earth banks and wooden palisades, home to perhaps 500 soldiers. Despite its modest size and temporary nature, the fort served its purpose and provided security in the form of a permanent garrison. It was to be 60 years before a more solid and long-lasting military fortification was built.

The fort that we are today able to explore was built, like the later wall around London, of a type of limestone known as Kentish ragstone. This came, as the name suggests, from Kent. It was quarried near the modern town of Maidstone and then transported by ship along the River Medway until it flowed into the Thames Estuary. From there, the ships travelled upstream to Londinium. We can be sure that this was the route by which the stone reached London for two reasons. The first of these is a simple matter of logistics. Such vast amounts of stone were used in building projects such as the fort and later London Wall that it would have been hugely impractical to bring it from Kent in horses and carts. Building the wall alone required somewhere in the region of 85,000 tons of stone, which translates into about 3,000 shiploads. The number of horses and carts which would be needed for such a project between Maidstone and London beggars the imagination! There is another reason that we know that boats were used to transport the material used to build the fort and wall, and this is that one of them, still with its cargo, was found in the Thames.

In September 1962 a shipwreck was found near Blackfriars Bridge, while work was being carried out on a new river wall. It proved to be the oldest seafaring vessel ever found in Northern Europe and by happy chance it was possible to date its construction fairly accurately. When it was being built and the mast fitted, a coin was placed beneath the mast for good fortune. This was from the reign of the Emperor Domitian, who died in 96 AD. This suggests strongly that the ship was probably built around the beginning of the second century AD. When found, it still had a load of Kentish ragstone on board.

It is time to start exploring the fort and the best place to begin is at another bombsite, one which is similar in some ways to that which we looked at beside Huggin Hill. We begin at St Paul's Underground station, which is on the Central Line. On leaving the station at Exit 2, we cross Cheapside and walk up Foster Lane. On the right is a church with the peculiar name of St Vedast-alias-Foster. Walking a few yards past this brings us to a doorway, also on the right, which looks as though it is the private entrance to some garden. The blue-painted doors are usually open during the hours of daylight and this archway actually leads to a courtyard connected to the church.

This paved area, not much larger than the footprint of an average family home, was formerly part of the graveyard attached to the adjacent church. It is edged with shelters, putting one in mind of a miniature cloister, and there are benches to sit on and relax. All in all, it is one of the most peaceful and secluded spots in central London. It is also just the place to take the opportunity of touching with our own hands some tessellated flooring from a Roman building which stood not far from here. This section of paving is fixed to the wall of the church, to your right as you enter the courtyard. It has a curious pattern, consisting of interlocking circles and may be seen in Illustration 23. Like the other examples of mosaic flooring at which we have looked, it is made up of little reddish-brown, terracotta cubes.

We have remarked before on the number of churches in central London which seem to have been first erected on top of the remains of Roman buildings and this piece of flooring is just such a case. It was found 18ft below the Church of St Matthew in Friday Street, during demolition work in 1886. It will be recalled that we walked down Friday Street when visiting the site of the Roman baths at Huggin Hill. This is a chance to study as closely as you wish, the way in which such flooring was constructed. We are most of us familiar with the more ornate examples of Roman mosaic, but this kind of thing was far more commonly used as flooring and required no huge skill to lay. The average building in Londinium would have been more likely to

23. Roman pavement on display in Foster Lane.

feature a floor of this kind, rather than a polychromatic representation of Europa being carried off by a bull or something of that nature.

It is surprising to note that this 2,000-year-old piece of flooring is not the most ancient object on display in the courtyard. A few feet to the left of it is a block of sun-baked brick, set into a niche, which, on close examination, is found to be covered in lines of cuneiform writing. It is taken from a ziggurat, which is rather like a pyramid, which stood in Assyria 3,000 years ago. It was given to the rector of the church during the rebuilding of St Vedast-alias-Foster following the Blitz. The man who presented this peculiar artifact to the church was the archologist Sir Max Mallowan, who was of course married to mystery writer Agatha Christie.

We turn right on leaving the courtyard and continue walking down Foster Lane, towards the fort. Before reaching it though, there is another curious fragment of the Roman city to be seen. After passing a turning on the left called Carey Lane, we come to an imposing building on the right, which is Goldsmiths' Hall. This is the home of the Worshipful Company of Goldsmiths, which has had its headquarters on this spot since the fourteenth century. The present building, which opened in 1835, is the third hall on this site. Following the demolition of the previous building in 1829, foundations were being dug for the new building, when an interesting discovery was made. About 20ft below the present street level was found a stone altar, upon which was carved a strange figure, which bears an uncanny similarity to the so-called 'Hunter God' which was found in the well beneath Southwark Cathedral.

Beneath the altar were enormously strong foundations made of masonry which had been cemented together. So well-built were these walls and floors of a Roman building that gunpowder had to be used to blow them up, in order that the foundations of the new Goldsmiths' Hall could be properly laid. This has led to the theory that a temple once stood here. The altar is on display in the Court Room of Goldsmiths' Hall, to which general access is not allowed. However, there are regular open days when parties of the public are taken on guided tours of the building and it is perhaps worth trying to fit in this particular walk with such a tour. This provides an opportunity to see the altar.

We shall have more to say about the altar found beneath Goldsmiths' Hall in the chapter on religious practices in Londinium, but before leaving the subject we observe that from at least as far back as the thirteenth century, there has been a legend that a Roman temple dedicated to Diana stood on Ludgate Hill, roughly where St Paul's Cathedral is today. Some people have claimed that the figure on the altar at Goldsmiths' Hall is of Diana and a bronze figure of the goddess, dating back to the Roman period, was found a few streets away.

Continuing along Foster Lane, we come to a road running at right angles to Foster Lane. This is Gresham Street and if we cross the road, we will find that Foster Lane has now become Noble Street. On our right is a churchyard and on our left a church, that of St Anne and St Agnes. If we carry on walking along Noble Street we will come after a few yards to another bombsite on the left-hand side of the street. This is similar in some ways to the garden at which we looked, which clings to the hillside next to Huggin Hill.

We pause when we reach the bombsite and peer down to what were once the cellars of some old buildings destroyed during the Blitz on London, which took place on and off between 1940 and 1945. These buildings had their foundations deep below the current street level and were in fact built on top of a fragment of the Roman wall which once surrounded London. This is not the whole story though, not by a long chalk. It is here that archaeologist W.F. Grimes was able to confirm in 1947 what he had long suspected, which was the existence of a fort at this location, which has become known as the Cripplegate Fort.

The area in which the wall and turrets of the fort are exposed is sometimes overgrown with weeds, which can make it difficult to make out the details at which we are looking. Right beneath us, as we stand at this end of the bombsite, is one corner of the fort. This may be seen in Illustration 24. The corners of such Roman forts were rounded, in a way which has given rise to the colloquial term for such structures, which is 'playing card' forts. The curvature of the wall is clearly visible here. Each corner featured a turret, a small tower which could be accessed via a staircase. There were other such turrets at points along the wall of the fort and one such is visible a little further along. It may be seen in Illustration 25. Looking along the length of this sunken area, which stretches along Noble Street, it is fairly obvious that this was a section of London Wall; the base of the Roman wall can be clearly seen.

What gave Grimes the confirmation he needed that this was more than merely the wall around London may be seen when we look more closely at the turret beneath us. The Roman wall runs straight along Nobel Street, but from it, another section of wall can be seen to shoot off to the left, almost at a right angle, jutting out from the turret. Why

24. A corner turret of the Roman fort in Noble Street.

25. The foundation of a turret of the Roman fort.

on earth should a wall around a city change direction in this way at a sudden and abrupt angle? The answer is simple. When the wall was being built, it incorporated an existing structure, namely a fort, which then also formed part of the outer wall around the entire city. The fort was built first and then the city wall had to adapt to the walls around the fort. We can see how this was done when we look at a small section of the wall in Noble Street. This is shown in Illustration 26.

When the wall was being built around Londinium, it was decided to make it about 20ft high and 8 or 9ft thick at the base. This created a slight problem, for the fort was to be incorporated into the wall. It was thought that the easiest way of doing this, while ensuring that the outer wall was of a standard height and thickness, was to add to the wall inside the fort, to bring it up to the same height and strength as the rest of the city wall. Illustration 26 shows perfectly how this was done. At the top of the picture we can see the base of the fort wall,

26. How the fort wall was thickened when the city wall was built.

which was about 4ft thick. Then, next to that on the inside of the fort, is a much thicker section. This is the part added to make this bit of the fort's wall the same height as that in the rest of the city. It is possible to see clearly the gap between the fort wall and the newly-added part of the city wall.

Before going any further with our explorations, we might stop and ask ourselves what the purpose was of this fort. On the face of it, this question sounds faintly absurd. Obviously, since Boudicca sacked the city and utterly destroyed it around 60 AD, it made perfect sense to have a fort where soldiers could be stationed who would defend Londinium against any further such military assault. This is plausible, although quite incorrect. In fact, the soldiers who lived in the barracks within this 12-acre fort were never intended to fight anybody, nor were they held in reserve, just on the off-chance that some other leader like Boudicca would emerge and menace the capital of the province. They served quite another purpose.

By the time that the fort at which we are looking came to be built, around 110 or 120 AD, Britain was at peace and there was no sign of internal rebellion or strife. London was a prosperous and orderly place and the Britons themselves were becoming, as one might say, 'Romanized'. Many wore togas in the city and, like the Romans, they were in the habit of using the public bathhouse. Roman culture had been found to be a good thing and the country was at peace. It was at this time that the fort was built in Londinium, some distance from where everybody else was living. It has been suggested that it was a visit by the Emperor Hadrian which precipitated the decision to construct an army base from stone in this way.

Today, we are familiar with the name of Hadrian due to the wall which he ordered to be built, to separate the Roman province from the barbarians who lived in what is now Scotland. In 122, the Emperor Hadrian arrived in Britain as part of a tour which he was making of the western provinces of the Roman Empire. London was spruced up at this time, in anticipation of the visit by Hadrian and certainly the fort was built at about this time. It is thought that Hadrian would not have been pleased to see soldiers being billeted with civilians and living cheek by jowl with everybody else in the city. The emperor was a man who had strict ideas about keeping the army as a respected institution which held itself a little aloof from the ordinary population. According to this theory, it was to avoid offending Hadrian that the huge enterprise of bringing in boatloads of quarried stone from Kent to build a fort in the proper Roman style was undertaken.

We remarked above that the purpose of the fort was not defensive and indeed we can even say that it was not primarily a military structure at all, despite the soldiers living in barracks. These men were for the most part administrators, somewhat akin to civil servants. Others had ceremonial duties, rather like those undertaken by the Household Cavalry who stand guard in London's Whitehall or the red-coated soldiers who guard Buckingham Palace. The main role of these men is to look impressive, rather than to actually guard anything or fight anybody. The governor of Londinium would expect to have a smart squad of such ceremonial troops at his headquarters. They could also have served as a bodyguard for the governor, if he visited anywhere outside Londinium.

We are able to make a shrewd guess about the duties of the troops in the fort because the tombstone erected above the grave of one of the officers at that time is displayed in the Museum of London. It is the first depiction of a Londoner that we have, and we can learn quite a bit from it.

In the later years of Londinium's existence, a century or so after the city wall had been built, it was decided to add semi-circular bastions, each of which would hold a giant crossbow-like weapon called a ballista. These were the Roman equivalent of artillery or heavy machine guns. There were at least twenty-two of these fearsome devices, which were capable of hurling huge arrows, each one the size of a spear, a distance of over half a mile. That these defences were built swiftly and as a matter of urgency, can be seen from the fact that both the riverside wall and the bastions made free use of stonework from graves, temples and monumental arches. It was as though a desperate situation required scavenging and looting stone from any available source. We can see this clearly if we compare a section of the original wall, built about the end of the second century AD, and a part of the river wall, which was constructed between 100 and 150 years later. Illustration 27 shows a section of the original wall and it will be seen that it is a beautiful piece of work. Meanwhile, Illustration 28 shows a bit of the later river wall and this has been cobbled together of all kinds of odd pieces of stone, including fragments of monumental archways, statues and gravestones.

When archaeological excavations took place along the line of the Roman wall at Camomile Street, the remains of one of the bastions mentioned above were discovered. This had been constructed from various pieces of stone, some of it from monuments which almost

27. The workmanship of the city wall.

28. The riverside wall.

certainly stood in the burial ground outside the walls of Londinium, roughly where the street of Bishopsgate now lies. This soldier is shown in Illustration 29. What is interesting is that although he is unmistakably a soldier, he is carrying scrolls and writing materials, rather than weapons of war. This strongly suggests that this soldier, who probably died in the first century AD, was a clerical administrator rather than a man of action. The gravestone may be seen in the Museum of London.

Returning now to the south-west corner of the fort, where we are standing, it will be seen that the line of the fort wall runs towards us along Noble Street and then curves round at the corner below us. The curvature of the corner of the wall may be seen in Illustration 24 (see page 76). The walls of the fort were probably around 15ft high and had a sentry walk at the top, which could be reached from staircases in turrets. We know too that the walls were roughly 4ft thick. Later

29. Statue of a soldier, from a tombstone.

on, we shall be looking at the foundation of one of walls and we can, if we wish, measure them for ourselves.

We walk along Noble Street, with the bombsite on our left. It is curious to reflect that during the years following the end of the Second World War, empty spaces like this were common all over London, but this is the last remaining example. It will be seen that broken–down and derelict buildings run along the site and that these are built upon the remnants of the fort's wall. A little way along, two parallel lines of masonry jut out from the wall. These are the foundations of another of the turrets, similar to that which stood at the corner.

Noble Street ends at the road known as London Wall and it is necessary to cross the road in order to follow the line of the wall to the next visible parts. Once we have crossed London Wall, be see immediately in front of us, a road sign bearing the name of the thoroughfare. To the left of this is an unobtrusive concrete stairwell, leading down to the ground level of Londinium. At the foot of the stairs, we find that we are near the entrance to an underground car park and metal doors which lead to a fascinating relic of Roman London. It is the west gate which once led into the fort which we are exploring. It is not easy to gain access to these remains, which are under the control of the City of London. The Museum of London sometimes arranges open days here, but these are erratic and it is impossible to predict when they are likely to be held. Readers wishing to visit the site will have to do some research of their own to find out when next it is possible to pass through the doorway and view the best-preserved part of the fort.

What can be seen here are the foundations of the gateway into the fort and the guardhouse which stood alongside it. The fort was square and there was a gate like this in each of the four walls. These served rather like a modern-day security check, a bit like the entrance to Downing Street, say. Soldiers were stationed in the guardhouse to ensure that anybody entering the fort had proper business there. They would also be able to make sure that no soldiers were slipping out when they were supposed to be on duty inside the fort. One interesting feature of the masonry which we can see here is the original wall of the fort and the way that it was strengthened when the wall was built around the city, 70 or 80 years after the fort had been constructed. We saw this same feature in Noble Street.

Near the foot of the stairs which we descended from London Wall is a tall and imposing derelict brick structure. This was once a medieval bastion of London Wall, with later brickwork built above it. The foundations of a masonry wall run across this bastion and they may be seen in Illustration 30. We see here, even more clearly, the same thing which may be observed in the section of wall hidden under the

30. The foundation of the fort wall and later city wall.

carpark. If you look at Illustration 30, you will that to the left is the remains or foundations of the fort wall, with a gap running alongside it, and more masonry beyond that. The neatly delineated wall on the left is the original wall of the fort, which was only 3 or 4ft thick. When the city wall was built and two walls of the fort consequently became part of the outer defences of the city, then those walls were reinforced and made as thick and tall as the rest of London Wall. This was done by building the new wall inside the old one and joining the two together. This accounts for that narrow space seen in Illustration 30, where the two walls meet. This may be compared with the bit of the wall seen in Illustration 26 (see page 77), which shows the same thing.

There are more parts of the fort to see and if we walk now across the grass and away from the main road of London Wall, we shall be able to follow the line of the fort wall, as it heads towards the concrete housing estate known as Barbican. A close look at the wall on our left as we walk past it will reveal that although it is constructed from ordinary bricks, it has been built upon the foundations of the Roman wall. We can see the course of tiles used by the Roman when building the wall. Carry on in a straight line, always following the line of the wall, and we come to another medieval bastion, although there is no trace of Roman masonry to be seen here. Pass this on your right and continue towards the long pond ahead.

We come to the last of the medieval bastions at this point, which overlooks the water. This marks the corner of the fort and so we know that from the corner turret at which we looked in Noble Street, to the point where we now are, we have walked the entire length of one of the walls of the fort. Our way is now blocked by some black-painted metal railings, but if we look through them to the right, we can just see in the distance another stretch of the wall. This is the north wall of the fort, but to reach it will mean retracing our steps a little. If we walk back to the foot of the stairs which we descended to reach here, we will look at the next part of the fort wall which is still standing.

When you reach the car park at which we looked earlier, turn left and walk up the slope towards the road called London Wall. Then turn left and walk along it. You will soon come to a flight of stairs on your left, leading down to some houses and flats. Above the stairs is a sign saying '80 London Wall'. Walk down the stairs and then continue across an area where some cars are parked, and with a garden on your left. This is Monkwell Square. Turn right when you reach a line of buildings. This will bring you out into a street called Wood Street and if you turn left, it will take you towards a tall block of flats. Before walking towards them, we pause and reflect that we are now on the site of one of the fort's entrances, in the north wall, and that after the city wall was built this became a gate not just to enter the fort, but into the city itself. It was known in later years as Cripplegate and this is the reason that the fort is sometimes referred to as the Cripplegate Fort. The other gateway of the fort which was on the city wall when it was completed, the west gate that we passed, was walled up at some point. Bollards block the way to ordinary traffic and beyond them is a restaurant called the Wood Street Bar. Walk towards this and then turn left, which will bring you into an open space which is dominated by an old church, St Giles Cripplegate.

The church of St Giles is beside a modest lake, overlooked by a block of flats. This little lake or pond lies just where the external ditch would have been, outside the Roman city wall. If you walk up to the railings overlooking this little lake, you will see straight in front of you a stretch of the old London Wall. This was originally part of the north wall of the fort, although most of the upper sections are of later, medieval construction. We are outside the city now and the lowest parts of this wall are the parts of the fort which faced outward. It may be seen in Illustration 31.

31. A section of the wall near St Giles Cripplegate Church.

There is one final section of the fort wall to see. It is probably wearisome for readers to keep being told to retrace their steps, but the Barbican development, where we currently are, is something of a maze and very difficult to find one's way around. Short cuts are few and far between and it is easier by far simply to stick to streets with recognizable names. If readers will now retrace their steps along Wood Street, to the point where they entered it from Monkwell Square, then they will see on the opposite side of Wood Street a small road called St Alphage Garden. Walking long this for a few yards will bring us to another section of the London Wall on our left. This is set in two gardens, one at this level and another, on the other side of the wall, which is at the old Roman street level.

The section of wall which we first see is largely from the medieval period. The upper part if made of brick and the crenelations make it look like part of a castle. It is worth spending a little time looking at the wall from this level, if only out of interest in the past. To see the original wall of the fort though, it is necessary to walk down some steps and enter Salter's Garden. This is usually open to the public on weekdays. This area is roughly at the ground level of Roman London and the lower part of the wall which we can see here is from that time. This is the outer wall of the fort. Illustration 32 shows what it looks like today.

This is, alas, the final part of the fort which is open to view. The foundations of some of the barracks and also a couple of short pieces of the outer wall have been uncovered during building work, but have been left undisturbed and built over. In the course of this walk, we have looked at every part of the fort which is still visible. It is time now to look at the wall which was built around the entire city at the end of the second or beginning of the third century AD. This walk is a fairly lengthy one, although it may of course be undertaken a bit at a time rather than all in one go.

32. St Alphage.

Chapter 8

London's Wall

The most obvious and visible remains of Roman London in the modern city are the stretches of wall which are scattered in a wide arc from the Tower of London to the vicinity of St Paul's Cathedral. We have already looked at a few of these, the ones which were originally part of the walls of the fort.

Nobody quite knows why it was decided towards the end of the second century AD to build a huge wall encircling the 300 acres or so which was the extent of Londinium at that time. The seemingly obvious answer is that it was to protect the city from attack by some outside force. It may have been something to do with a struggle for power within the Roman Empire or perhaps it was just felt to be fitting that such an important city as this *should* have a wall around it. At one time it was believed that the wall had been thrown up hastily when Clodius Albinus, a governor of Britain, took his army to the Continent in order to launch a bid to become emperor. This seems improbable, for the wall was a massive and well-planned operation. There is no sign of haste about its construction, unlike the river wall which was built many years later. The landward wall needed a million blocks of stone, weighing a total of 85,000 tons, and so meticulously was it built that even today it looks as though it might easily last for another 2,000 years. Illustration 27 (see page 80) shows a small section of the Roman wall and it will be seen how neatly it has been constructed.

There is another possible reason for going to all the trouble of building this huge structure and that is that it was not motivated by military considerations at all but was rather designed to make it easier to levy taxes and customs duties. Not all walls are defensive. One remembers, for instance, the wall which once encircled West Berlin. This was not intended to prevent incursions by armed attackers; it had quite a different purpose. Without understanding the historical context, it can difficult to work out the true significance of a wall. In the case of the Roman wall which surrounded Londinium, there may have been several reasons for building it. One of these could concern the fact that almost anything which was imported into, or exported from, Britain had to pass through the port in Londinium. The Thames faces the Rhine across the North Sea and almost all goods entered or left the province via that route. This is quite logical. This is where the traders and businessmen were. It was the simplest and most direct way of transporting anything to and from Europe.

The financial success of Britain as a province relied upon those in charge being able to tax goods and take a percentage of their value, to be used towards the running costs of the army and so on. Think for a moment about the purpose of modern borders between countries. These are seldom heavily fortified and intended to act as physical barriers to troops or tanks. Rather, they are typically symbolic; strips of barbed-wire fence and so on. The aim is not to block the advance of an army, but to ensure that heavily-laden lorries bringing alcohol, tobacco and anything else into the country must use designated crossing points, so that the goods they carry may be subject to inspection by customs officers. It may well be that the gates in the wall around London served a similar purpose during the third century AD.

Even so, the 20ft-high wall might look a little like overkill if it were only supposed to tackle smuggling. Perhaps there was more than one motive for going to the trouble of such a massive project. With the empire already facing rival contenders for the throne, perhaps it was felt that it would be no bad thing for this city at least to be secure from attack by some faction hoping to establish itself as the real power in the Roman Empire. Perhaps whoever caused it to be built wanted both to ensure the financial viability of Britain by making sure that all taxes and tolls were paid, while at the same time protecting the capital from some other upstart claimant to the throne?

We will probably never be able to divine for certain the motives which impelled those who had the wall built. We can however date the building of the wall to within 30 years, because of coins which have been found. It could not have been built earlier than 190 AD nor later that 225 AD. It is for this reason that we know that it was being built about the time that Clodius Albinus was governor, for he ruled from 193 to 197 AD. His attempt to be emperor was ultimately crushed when Septimius Severus defeated him in battle and became emperor himself, so it is possible that it was Severus and not the former governor who decided that the wall should be erected.

We shall trace the line of the wall on foot and so begin where the first visible part of the Roman wall is to be found, within the grounds of the Tower of London. This is a small section, only a few feet high, which is near the White Tower. It may be seen in Illustration 33. The Tower of

33. Part of the city wall within the Tower of London.

London was built across the line of the Roman wall, which explains how this isolated fragment ended up wholly enclosed within it.

While we are in the grounds of the Tower, it is worth examining a section of Roman wall which was built long after the one whose course we shall be tracing. This known as the Riverside Wall. When the first part of the wall was built, the three miles or so which surrounded Londinium, the only hazard was likely to be from the land. Rome, after all, ruled the seas and there was no risk of any hostile vessels slipping up the Thames to assault the city. This changed though as the empire weakened, and there grew a danger from pirates and irregular forces from northern Europe, such as the Saxons. In the late third and early fourth century AD, about a hundred years after the main wall was built, a second one was erected along the riverbank, to protect London against attack by forces sailing up the Thames from the North Sea. It was a hastily constructed and extremely shoddy piece of work.

If you go to the shop which is on the south side of the White Tower, near to where the cages for the ravens are found, then in front of it you will find uncovered a length of the riverside wall. It really is a wretched piece of work, when compared with the landward wall. Different-sized pieces of stone, chunks of old masonry from temples, lumps of chalk, all stuck together any old how. Illustration 28 (see page 81) shows the riverside wall at this point. The foundations for this wall were sometimes made of wooden stakes, and at other times the wall would simply be build straight onto the earth, without worrying about any foundations at all. The contrast between this barrier, which was obviously a rush job in response to an emergency of some kind, and the beautifully-finished work of the first part of the wall could hardly be greater. It is now time to look at perhaps the best-preserved piece of Roman building in the City of London.

On leaving the Tower of London, we make our way to Tower Hill Tube station and there, right by the entrance, stands a magnificent example of Roman skill at producing structures which were built to last. When similar sections of the wall were blocking the route planned for the Circle Line in the late nineteenth century, it was thought that a gang of workmen wielding pickaxes and hammers would soon be able to reduce it to rubble. It proved too hard a task and the railway company was forced to resort instead to the use of gunpowder.

Illustration 27 (see page 80) is of a section of the wall at Tower Hill. It will be observed that the blocks of stone are neatly squared off and laid in courses like bricks. It is very different in appearance to the bit of the riverside wall at which we looked in the precincts of the Tower of London. In the photograph taken at Tower Hill, it will be seen that for every few feet in height, there are lines of tiles built into the wall. It is sometimes thought that these are some decorative effect, but in fact they are an integral part of the method used in ensuring that the wall would be so solid and resistant to damage.

The first step was to prepare solid foundations of clay mixed with flint. On this, two walls were built of stone blocks cut out of Kentish ragstone, running parallel with a space between them of some 6ft. The first line of blocks were not ragstone, but rather very neatly squared-off sections of red sandstone, which formed a decorative plinth for the side of the wall which faced outwards. This would then be filled with pieces of stone mixed with mortar, to form a solid core. After a height of 5 or 6ft was reached, then two or three layers of roof tiles would be cemented over the top of the core and incorporated into the walls. These were carefully laid so that they were level and sealed in the core. Then another half-dozen courses of the two walls would be laid and, as before, the space between them was filled with the same rubble and mortar as before. Following this, tiles would be laid over this as well and the process repeated until the wall was about 20ft high. A deep ditch was dug outside the wall, as an added impediment to anybody minded to attack, and the earth from this excavation was piled up against the inner part of the wall.

The wall at Tower Hill really is an impressive sight, soaring to about 35ft in height. Illustration 2 (see page ix) shows this part of the wall.

Only the first 15ft is Roman though, the rest of it dating from medieval work which was carried out to enlarge the wall around London. This bit of the wall is a good place to examine the construction in detail, because it is possible to see a cross section of the Roman wall, which gives us one clue as to why it was so tremendously strong. When we cement bricks or pieces of stone together these days, the mortar is a smooth paste which consists of nothing more than a mixture of sand and cement. If we look closely at the mortar which, together with the chunks of stone, made up the core of the Roman wall, we will see that it contained stones, grit and other hard material. Looking at the core of the wall now, it comes as no surprise that at times explosives were needed to demolish masonry structures dating from that time.

The wall which stands at Tower Hill is separated by only a matter of yards from the next stretch, which is not immediately visible. If you stand at the end of the wall which is furthest from the Tower of London, visible in the distance, you can follow the line of sight from that vantage point and walk along a space between buildings, which is lined with planters. After a few feet, this will bring you to where the wall continues. This part too is some 35ft high and the Roman portion, the first 15ft of it from the ground upwards, is very well preserved. To see clearly, you will need to lean over some railings and look down. The wall continues in the same direction, but to see the rest of it, you will need to go back the way you came and when you reach the end of the section of wall at Tower Hill Tube station, you must turn left and walk a little way, until you come to a path between two buildings which are called the London Suite. This leads to a square called the Crescent. Upon leaving this, keep an eye out for a narrow alleyway on the left, which will lead you to a substantial stretch of the wall which is completely hidden from view by the surrounding buildings.

The bit of Roman wall standing outside Tower Hill Tube station might not inaptly be described as the public face of London's Roman wall. It is the bit seen by tourists and many photographs are taken of people posing in front of it. The section at which we are now looking is longer and more interesting, although it is very rare to see a single tourist or sightseer here. This part of the wall can be seen in Illustration 34.

This part of the wall is as high as that at Tower Hill, rising about 35ft from the base, which is below ground level, to the top. Most of what can be seen at first glance is medieval, including the slits for archers to shoot from. It is a testament to the solidity of the Roman masonry and foundations that in the Middle Ages it proved possible to build another 20ft of wall directly onto the Roman part and that the added weight did not adversely affect the stability of the original structure. The Romans in London built to last!

34. The wall at Cooper's Row.

To see the Roman part of the wall, it is necessary to peer over the railings at the lowest 15ft of the wall, from the Roman ground level up. It is possible in this part of the wall to observe something which is missing from the more public section at Tower Hill, and that is the decorative red sandstone plinth which once ran along the bottom of the Roman wall. It is not possible to get very close to the Roman portions here and you must crane your head around to get a good view.

Before moving onto the next bit of the wall, a few words need to be said about the alterations which were made in the third and fourth centuries AD. It will be recalled that there exists some doubt as to the actual reason for building the wall around Londinium in the first place. There can be no doubt though as to its later importance as a purely military structure. We looked at part of the riverside wall in the grounds of the Tower of London and this shows every sign of having been hastily thrown up to meet some pressing emergency. Compare, once more, the part of the riverside wall shown in Illustration 28 with the original landward wall in Illustration 27 (see pages 80 and 81). It can be seen at once that the first wall was built in a very methodical and planned fashion, but that the second wall along the riverfront was just composed of anything which came to hand. The fear, most likely, was that irregular naval forces, pirates and brigands sailing from the North Sea, would slip up the Thames Estuary and attack the city. This wall is intended to defend from attack from the water.

About 50 years or more after the riverside wall sprang up, modifications were made to the landward wall. These works consisted of building twenty bastions on the eastern side of the wall, once again indicating the direction from which the supposed threat might come. The bastions were semi-circular towers which jutted out from the wall and could be accessed at the top from the sentry walk which ran along the top of the wall. When we explored the fort in Chapter 3, we looked at some medieval bastions of broadly similar design. These were, however, hollow, whereas the ones built by the Romans were solid. They needed to be very strong, because the purpose of these towers was to hold a ballista. That the towers, with their fearsome catapults capable of hurling iron-tipped bolts the size of spears for hundreds of yards, were built as a matter of urgency can be seen from the material used in their construction. The riverside wall was made up of all kinds of blocks of stone which were at one time treated with reverence. For instance, altars from temples and also images of deities were shoved into the mud, along with large fragments of monumental arches. When the bastions were being put together, a solid core was needed and so the builders cast around for any big pieces of stone which had not been used for the wall along the waterfront. They realized that burial grounds provided a rich source of such material and so began breaking up monuments and tombs to provide the filling for the new towers. In Chapter 7, we saw how the monument to a Roman officer had been recovered from such a bastion in Camomile Street. The same thing happened with the next part of the wall we shall visit, which includes the foundations of one of those turrets added to the wall in the fourth century.

On leaving the alleyway into which we walked to see the last bit of the wall, we turn left, until we come to a road. On the right, see a large and prominent sign which declares that this is No. 2 America Square. On our left is a conference centre which is No. 1 America Square. When the foundations were being dug here, a stretch of the Roman wall more than 100ft in length was found. Had this been chanced upon during the Victorian period, it would most likely have been smashed to pieces and used for builders' rubble, but in these more enlightened times it has been carefully preserved. The wall is complete with the red sandstone base at which we looked in the last section of the wall which we visited. In the conference centre, this wall now forms a most impressive backdrop to one of the larger rooms.

It is worth asking at the reception of this building if it might be possible to visit the wall here and just have a look at it. If there is no function there and the receptionist is not too busy, you may be lucky. Otherwise, it is always possible, at any time of the day or night, to see at least part of the wall. The street which we have come to is called Crossway and if we look at that part of No. 1 America Square which faces Crossway, we will see that over the top of a low wall, windows allow us to see down into the basement. There we can see just the top of a bit of the Roman wall.

We now cross the road and walk along Vine Street. After a few yards, you will come, on your left, to a very modern building which provides student accommodation. Through the large plate-glass windows, you will see a part of the Roman wall, with the foundations of a bastion. This is shown in Illustration 35. It is claimed that the remains of the wall here will at some future time be open to the public, but at the time of writing, the winter of 2022, it was not possible to enter the building to see them close up. They are however visible through the large glass windows. What we can see is a short part of the wall, the lowest bit of which is Roman, with medieval stonework above it. Most interestingly

35. The foundation of a Roman bastion of the city wall.

though, we can see the foundations of one of the bastions about which we have been talking. This is semi-circular and juts out from the wall. When this was excavated, it was found that, just as with other bastions, this one had used as rubble for the core, old tombstones. One of a 10-year-old girl called Marciana was unearthed.

Most cultures have some kind of respect for memorials and graves and the Romans who lived in London at that time were no exception. It is perhaps an indication of the crisis which they felt themselves to be facing that they should not hesitate to pull down temples and tombs and incorporate them into a project of this kind. The most noticeable feature of the foundations of the bastion at Vine Street is that they are gleaming white. This is because as well as chunks of masonry, blocks of chalk were also used to make up the solid core of the structure. Just across the river, at Greenwich, are chalk escarpments from which the material could have been quarried and brought across the bridge. Mining chalk is a lot quicker and easier than digging up and cutting to shape harder stone, such as the ragstone which was transported from Kent. The amount of stone and chalk which would have been needed to build a solid tower of this size was simply immense and perhaps it is not surprising that the builders were driven in desperation to looting bits of stone from wherever they could lay their hands upon it.

A quick calculation gives us some idea how much stone would have been necessary to build those towers to hold the catapults. They were as high as the wall itself, which was about 20ft. Each bastion was roughly 10ft deep by 10ft wide, giving a base area of perhaps 100ft^2. This would give a volume of 2,000ft^3, which would need to be filled with stone and mortar. If we assume, which is generally thought to be the case, that there were twenty-two bastions on the east side of the city wall, then this would mean that something like 44,000ft^3 of stone would be needed to build them. That really is an awful lot of material to find and we can hardly be surprised that the Romans turned their attentions to temples, monumental arches and any other source of stone.

It is possible, by working one's way around the outside of the building, to gain some spectacular views of the wall and bastion. One notable feature of the wall is that the sandstone plinth is intact and in its original position. It will be seen how this formed the first layer of blocks when constructing the wall which would face outwards to the world. Those bits of red sandstone, which we are looking down at from our vantage point, show us the ground level of Roman London.

After we have finished looking at this particularly interesting part of the wall, we continue down Vine Street, until we come to India Street, which cuts across it. Turn left and then immediately right and you will find yourself in the street called Jewry. There are several sections of the Roman wall in this street, but they are in the basements of private properties and viewing them is wholly contingent upon the goodwill of the owners of the buildings. The first may be found in the basement of the David Game College, which is the first building on your right after entering Jewry. Some of the other buildings in this row also have small fragments of the Roman wall in their cellars, but the Three Tuns public house has a fairly long bit, which can be seen for the price of a drink.

We reach a main road now, which was the site of Aldgate, one of the gates leading into Londinium. Cross over and head up Duke's Place and then Bevis Marks. These roads run precisely along the line of the Roman wall. On our right, behind the buildings, is another road which is parallel to the one along which we are walking. This is called Houndsditch, and it is where the ditch outside the city wall once was. In the late sixteenth century, historian John Stow wrote that it acquired this name because the ditch became used as a general dumping ground for any and all unwanted refuse, including dead dogs. Curiously enough, excavations there have found the skeletons of dogs in the ditch which date from the time of the Romans, so perhaps it was known by the Latin equivalent of Houndsditch at that time too.

Bevis Marks becomes Camomile Street shortly before we come to the main road of Bishopsgate. There was another gate here in Roman

London and to the right was a huge burial ground, which covered the area on either side of the road from the north which passed through the gate. If we cross over and carry on in the same direction, we find that we are on the aptly-named London Wall, which does indeed follow the line of the old wall. Crossing the road, we come to the church of All-Hallows-on-the-Wall. This was built on the wall and part of the old medieval city wall may be seen in the churchyard. This wall was built on top of the Roman one, which still lies beneath the ground here. The vestry of All-Hallows-on-the-Wall is circular and it is built on one of the Roman bastions which stood here. Because of the peculiar relationship between the church, the vestry and the wall, the pulpit of this church cannot be accessed from the nave, but can only be reached by leaving the main body of the church and going into the vestry. If we turn and face the church, then it is just possible to see the curved wall of the vestry, which follows the foundations of the bastion.

We carry on walking along London Wall, which veers a little to the left. We are still following the line of the Roman wall, as will shortly be seen. We proceed along this street until we see that a large building ahead of us, that the road must pass beneath. On the right is the section of the wall in St Alphage Garden at which we looked when we examined the remains of the fort. We pass too the ruins of an old church. Just after this, a ramp will be seen on the right-hand side, which leads down to an underground car park. It is flanked by no-entry signs, but these apply only to vehicles. It is time to see perhaps the strangest surviving piece of the Roman wall.

At the bottom of the ramp, one turns left and walks past an office containing security staff. They are used to visitors who wish to see the Roman wall. It is a little walk along the underground car park, until you reach Bay 52 and there, standing right in the middle of a parking space, is a perfectly preserved section of the wall, which may be seen in Illustration 36. Unlike many of the bits of the wall at which we have looked, this is entirely Roman, with no medieval additions. It was uncovered in 1957, when land around here was being cleared

36. An underground part of the Roman wall.

of the devastation wrought during the Blitz. It is certainly a surreal sight, to see it standing here among the smooth, bare concrete walls of a modern car park.

Leave the car park by the same route by which it was entered and then carry on walking along London Wall in the same direction that we were travelling before. After passing beneath the building, we emerge into the open once more and see a footbridge crossing the road above us. Just before this, we cross the road and take the turning on the left, which is Noble Street.

We of course passed up this street in the other direction when we explored the fort in Chapter 7. On our right are the remains of the city wall, which was combined at this point with the wall of the fort. At the end of this old bombsite, we come to the square foundation of one of the turrets which stood at each corner of the fort. We can trace the curving wall which formed the corner of the fort, noting that it is

37. The city wall meets the fort.

about 4ft thick. At right angles to the turret is a much thicker and more solidly constructed foundation. This can be seen in Illustration 37. This is the city wall, which was being built around Londinium and which reached the fort at this point and then took a sharp left turn. To see what else is still visible of the Roman wall, we need to follow the line of this foundation. To do this, we have to walk along Gresham Street for a short distance, until we come to Aldersgate. If we now turn right and cross the road, then we will come to the entrance of a churchyard.

We have come to one of the curiosities of London, a place called Postman's Park. Beneath a little arcade are plaques which commemorate ordinary people who gave their lives to save others. This is not, however, the main interest that this miniature garden holds for us. If we turn left after entering Postman's Park, we will see a building on our left which is separated from the churchyard by a line of black railings. Looking over the railings will show a drop of perhaps 20ft leading to and open area which gives light to the basement windows. A long part of the Roman wall lies beneath us and runs along the bottom of the railings. Unfortunately, it is obscured from view and however much one leans over, it is not possible to see the wall. It is visible to those looking out of those windows below us, but impossible for us to view.

Passing through Postman's Park, we come to St Bartholomew's Hospital and cannot follow the wall beneath that. Instead, turn left into King Edward Street and cross the road. We can pick up the wall again after it leaves the hospital. You will come to a ruined church on the right, which has now been turned into another of those little gardens which we find scattered here and there across the City of London. Just before this, is a pedestrian walkway leading to a building which proclaims itself to be American bank Merrill Lynch. In their basement is a very fine piece of the Roman wall, with a bastion attached to it. It was at one time thought that this was one of the original Roman bastions, but this has proved not to be the case. It is instead from the medieval period.

During building work here in the early part of the twentieth century, a stretch of the Roman city wall was found, together with a semi-circular bastion, which was thought to be part of the fortifications added to the wall a century or two after it was built. These remains were preserved in the basement of the building, part of the General Post Office, but were not accessible to the public. This changed when the original building on the site was demolished and the site acquired by the Merrill Lynch group. Part of the planning permission for the new office block was that the Roman wall and bastion should be opened to the public and that a small museum should be constructed in the basement for this purpose.

While the foundations for the building were being constructed, archaeologists from the Museum of London worked on the wall and bastion, finding out as much as possible. One thing which they soon discovered was that this was no Roman structure. The wall itself was certainly Roman, but the bastion dated from the medieval period. This presented something of a mystery, because it did not look as though it was part of a defensive fortification, like the other bastions which are found along the east side of the city wall. Eventually, they concluded that the most likely explanation was that the Roman wall had been built on marshy and unstable ground here and that it had begun to lean a little. The bastion probably served to prop it up and prevent it from keeling over.

The next piece of the Roman wall which is preserved may be seen inside the Old Bailey courtroom, across the road. Because of security considerations though, it can only be seen on pre-booked guided tours. A gate stood roughly where the Old Bailey is today in Roman times. There is one more section of the wall to be seen, although it is technically on private property. It is unlikely though that anybody will object if people wish simply to look at this curiosity. Cross the road and walk towards the Old Bailey. Before reaching it, there is a turning on the left called Warwick Lane. Walk down this street, noting on the right the imposing wooden doors through which prisoners on trial at the Old Bailey pass to and from their way to prison. You will come to a turning on the right called Amen Corner. This leads to a private garden and a group of houses called Amen Court. The entrance is blocked to traffic by a yellow-and-black-striped pole, but it is easy enough to duck under this and walk to the wall at the end, beside which is a flower bed. Most of the wall is made up of brickwork, but in two places, it can be seen to be built over some structure composed of ragstone. This is tiny fragment of London Wall. There is some debate about whether this is part of the rubble core of the topmost part of the Roman wall, or rather a bit of the medieval wall built above the Roman one. This may be seen in Illustration 38.

If we leave Amen Court and walk back into Amen Corner and turn right when we come to Warwick Lane, we will soon find ourselves on Ludgate Hill. There is one final piece of the Roman wall which is

38. A section of the wall near St Paul's Cathedral.

sometimes accessible. Turn right onto Ludgate Hill and you will find yourself standing outside the church of St Martin within Ludgate. It is called that because this is the spot where the gate in the wall which became known as Ludgate was to be found, and the church was tucked just inside the wall. There is some debate as to whether the architect of the church, which was rebuilt after the Great Fire of London, was Christopher Wren or Robert Hooke. The tall, sharp spire was supposedly designed as a deliberate counterpont the dome of St Paul's on the crest of Ludgate Hill, but that may well be no more than an urban myth.

St Martin's is of interest to us because it was built right up against the city wall and in the crypt may be seen some of the Roman stonework of the wall, which has been incorporated into the foundations. It is sometime possible to be allowed to look at the crypt of the church, but more often than not, the doors are closed when one visits and it is not even possible to inspect the interior of the place, let alone petition for permission to descend into the crypt.

This is the last part of the Roman wall which is visible today. The wall ran south from here, across Ludgate Hill and down to the River Thames, but any remaining parts are still buried beneath the buildings which stand between here and the river.

We have so far in this book looked at the important and monumental structures of Roman London; the basilica, fort and city wall. It is time now to turn our attention from public architecture to private dwellings. It will perhaps come as a surprise to readers to learn that they are able to go underground and actually walk around two Roman houses in central London. Also within the wider bounds of Greater London is a country villa and this too may be visited.

Chapter 9

At Home with the First Londoners

I f the average person was called upon to describe the interior of a Roman house, it is altogether likely that he would describe mosaic floors with intricate, mythological scenes portrayed, elaborately painted walls and of course that most typical feature of Roman homes, the hypocaust, a central heating system which used hot air to warm the floors and walls of a house. We summon up such images from pictures in history books or reconstructions in museums. Of course, there *were* such homes in Roman London, but places of that kind would be the exception rather than the rule. Our perception is as distorted as if in a couple of thousand years' time, archaeologists were to excavate Buckingham Palace or perhaps the home of David and Victoria Beckham. Doing so would give quite a different view of domestic life in early twenty-first century Britain than if a dig had been conducted on a housing estate in East London.

There certainly *were* grand mosaic floors such as the Bucklersbury mosaic, which is shown in Illustration 39. This is used as part of a reconstruction of a Roman home which may be found in the Museum of London. Of course, this makes a very pleasing display and the mosaic floor really was dug up in London and had formed the floor of a domestic dwelling. It was, however, by no means typical of the kind of floor one would be likely to encounter on entering the home of the average Londoner 2,000 years ago.

Illustration 40 shows something a little more modest than the kind of Roman domestic interior that we usually see, but one far more likely to resemble the home of an ordinary person at that time. This is the floor uncovered in the crypt of the church All Hallows by the

39. A grand Roman mosaic in a domestic setting.

40. The pavement at All Hallows by the Tower.

41. Another part of the floor at All Hallows by the Tower.

Tower. We can see another part of the floor of the Roman house on the foundations of which this church was erected, in Illustration 41. One final example of a Roman floor *in situ* should be sufficient to make the point. In Illustration 16 (see page 40), we can see the floor found beneath St Bride's Church in Fleet Street. None of these floors, made of little cubes of baked clay laid in crooked and irregular lines, is especially attractive from an aesthetic viewpoint, but they were certainly durable and long lasting. Such floors could be made a little more attractive, even when the tesserae were all of one plain colour, by laying them in geometric patterns. We saw a section of such a floor in the courtyard next to the church of Saint Vedast-alias-Foster, near St Paul's Cathedral. This was, it will be recalled, found deep beneath a church in nearby Friday Street. The little cubes of clay are misshapen and irregular, but they are neatly arranged in two circles, which are just touching each other. It gives a pleasing impression. This is shown in Illustration 23 (see page 73).

The drab floors of the kind which we find beneath some London churches are not at all what most people visualize when thinking about Roman homes. Mind, even those plain little cubes of reddish-brown clay are an improvement on what many Londoners had to endure. Not everybody lived in houses built of stone, with a hypocaust to keep them warm. Many people lived in wattle and daub homes, essentially wooden frames smeared with clay. Others had wooden walls, filled in with bricks made of sun-dried mud to act as insulation. Instead of elaborate hypocausts, heating might be provided by a brazier of smouldering charcoal, something like a modern barbecue.

It is time to visit one or two Roman houses in London and get a feel for how Londoners of 2,000 years or so ago lived. The first home we shall visit is found in the most unexpected of places; somewhere one would never guess that a hidden archaeological treasure was to be found. This is the church of All Hallows by the Tower. To get there, we need to take a Tube train to Tower Hill Station, which is on the District and Circle Line. Before even leaving the station though, it is possible to see an unlikely piece of Roman history!

If you walk along the westbound platform at Tower Hill and look at the curved wall facing you across the railway tracks, you will eventually come upon what looks like a window, a square opening in the wall, so high up that you can barely see what lies beyond it. This may be seen in Illustration 42. When the Tube was built through this part of London, it had to cut through a formidable obstacle, which was a 75ft stretch of the Roman wall which lay in the path of the projected railway line. People were less concerned in Victorian London about preserving the past and when a stretch of old masonry was standing

42. Part of the Roman wall at Tower Hill Tube station.

in the way of industry and progress, then it had to go. Once the wall had been demolished and the station built, it was found that a tiny part was left, buried in the ground next to the westbound platform and so an aperture was made so that passengers waiting for a train could at least catch a fleeting glimpse of the past.

On leaving the station, we come to Trinity Gardens. In the distance may be seen the green spire of a church. This is our destination, All Hallows by the Tower. To reach it, we must walk through the gardens and then cross a busy road. Just after the end of the First World War a new vicar was appointed to this church. He was anxious, because he could hear the Tube trains rumbling beneath the place and feared the vibration might damage the fabric of the building. Because of this, he engaged surveyors to conduct explorations beneath the church, to check on the condition of the foundations. This was a stroke of luck, because it led to the discovery of a Roman house from the second century AD. It is this that we are about to visit.

On entering the church, we walk a few yards before turning to the right and heading for the steep stairs leading to the crypt. Before descending, it is worth pausing for a moment to look at the only part of a Saxon building which is still standing in the City of London. It is a massive arch, constructed of blocks of stone looted from nearby Roman buildings. The archway has no keystone and is partly constructed of reused tiles, which also date from the Roman period. The church was founded here in 675 AD, although the arch was probably not built until a few decades later. Like many of the other discoveries at which we have looked, this was revealed by the bombing of London during the Second World War. Until All Hallows by the Tower was ravaged by the explosions and fire of the Blitz, the Saxon arch had been bricked up, hidden inside a wall and forgotten. It is shown in Illustration 43.

The stairs to the crypt lead us down to the ground floor level of Roman London and glancing to the left, as soon as we reach the bottom of the stairs, reveals something quite extraordinary. We are now standing in a Roman house which dates from the second century AD. Unlike the floors of grand mansions or palaces, the floor of this home is not adorned with stunning mosaics with intricate geometrical designs or portraying mythological subjects. Instead, we see only a dingy, shabby stretch of pieces of broken terracotta tiles and pots, which have been laid on the bare earth. More than that, this floor is not smooth and level, as we expect those in our homes to be. Instead, it undulates and twists, like a carpet laid on an uneven surface. This is, at first, puzzling.

The earliest homes in Londinium were built of wood and they had floors of rammed earth. It was such houses which Boudicca and her army burned to the ground in 60 AD. When the city began to rise again, many people wanted something a little more comfortable than simple earthen floors. Few people could afford to engage craftsmen

43. The Saxon arch in All Hallows by the Tower church.

to design and install beautiful polychromatic mosaics to brighten up their home, such as the one we see in Illustration 39 (see page 109), but with a bit of thought, it was possible for the ordinary householder to improve a little on bare earth. The archetypal mosaic, of the kind with which we are familiar, is made up of little cubes, each about a centimetre on each side. These are made from stone, glass, fired clay and other substances and appear very smooth to the touch. Producing these cubes was time-consuming and therefore expensive, as was the technique used for laying them. We shall have more to say of this later, but it is enough for now to remember that such productions were likely to be beyond the reach of most ordinary citizens. There was an easier and cheaper DIY method. This entailed just finding bits of broken tiles and pottery which were roughly square and then pressing them straight into the earth. A smear of mortar between them and you had something which would be harder-wearing than a floor of earth and perhaps more attractive to the eye. Looking at the floor beneath the stairs at All Hallows by the Tower, you will see that many of these fragments of terracotta are not even square and they vary greatly in colour, some being almost black and others light grey. This is a far more typical, if less visually appealing, mosaic floor from Roman London than anything we are likely to see preserved in a museum.

The reason that this floor appears to be a little wavy, rather than completely flat, is quite simple. There was subsidence beneath Roman houses, just as there is sometimes under own dwellings. When you have a solid foundation, made of concrete, then this might crack if there is subsidence, but since this floor is just earth, it is flexible and able to bend and fold under pressure. The whitish streak running across the floor shows where a plaster wall once stood.

Perhaps fooling around with all those fiddly little bits of broken tiles proved too much of a chore for the person whose house this once was, because if you look at the floor which leads into the rest of the crypt, it is now possible to see another kind of floor, one which you will certainly never see in a museum. When the crypt was first being explored in the 1920s, some of the floors from the Roman house were found to be broken and in poor order. These were restored and the tiles re-laid and set firmly in a concrete base. They are still in their original position, although now securely set in place. The floor may be seen in Illustration 41 (see page 110). In addition to the tesserae laid in the same way as the floor at which we have just been looking, there is a different kind of surface, which consists of larger pieces of tiles, just old bits or half tiles of all different sizes, simply laid flat on the ground to provide something similar to crazy paving. These re-laid floors give us an opportunity which is not even afforded to those visiting famous Roman sites such as the city of Pompeii, because we are actually able to walk across the floor of a Roman house, in the very location where it was assembled almost 2,000 years ago.

A little way further into the crypt, on the right-hand side, is a glass cabinet showing various archaeological remains of a domestic nature which have been excavated in and around the church. Some of these undoubtedly belonged to the very people who laid the floor here. There is something fascinating about walking across the floor of the house which once stood here and then examining the everyday items which were used by those who lived here so long ago. Here are their pots and bowl, along with the little oil lamps by which they once illuminated their home. Here too is a miniature shrine, which would have been the centre of religious devotion. This is perhaps the only place in the whole of Britain where one may both visit a Roman home and at the same time examine the belongings of those who lived in it.

Opposite the case in which these relics of domestic life from Londinium may be seen is a marvellous diorama of Roman London, showing the city as it was at its height. This is well worth seeing for its own sake. One thing which the observant visitor will notice is that although the basilica, forum and fort are all present and in their correct positions, the amphitheatre is absent. This model was made long before its discovery in the 1980s. From the fact that the fort is included, we are able to guess that the model was made some time after the 1950s, when that part of Roman London was unearthed.

This then is the first of the Roman houses in London which we shall be visiting. It did not belong to anybody grand and important, but was certainly more typical of the way that the ordinary citizen would have been living than the reconstructed rooms in the Museum of London, for instance. There are two other houses which may be seen, one in central London and the other, although technically in London, was a country villa when it was built.

In Lower Thames Street, along the line of the riverbank in Roman times, stood a fine house. This was found in 1848, when the foundations were being excavated for the Coal Exchange. The discovery of the house, which had a private bathhouse attached to it, caused something of a stir in Victorian London and drawings of the remains appeared in the illustrated newspapers and magazines of the time. Fortunately, the walls and foundations of the buildings were not simply broken up and destroyed, as all too commonly happened when traces of Roman London were uncovered in those days. Instead, they were left intact beneath the Coal Exchange. When this was demolished in 1962, as part of a project to widen the road, the house was still there in the basement. It is now possible to visit it, although access is uncertain and irregular. It is, at the time of writing, limited to one or two days each week between April and November, although this may of course change in the future.

A flight of stairs leads down to the Roman ground level of 101 Lower Thames Street. The basement to which these stairs lead is stark and functional, being composed entirely of bare concrete columns and walls which support the weight of the building which stands overhead. A steel framework supports walkways which are suspended a few feet above the Roman house which we are visiting. It must be borne in mind that this site was on the very riverfront 2,000 years ago. The hillside which rises north towards Cornhill was cut into terraces, to provide a flat foundation for buildings such as this. The structure of the house at which we are looking is as follows. The main section runs parallel to the river and from either end protrudes a wing. These surrounded an open garden or courtyard which faces the river.

When this house was built, in the late second century AD, it would have been a fine property and owned by people of some standing. We know this because of the hypocaust which ran beneath it. A fire was maintained in a special furnace room and the hot air from this drawn under the floors and through terracotta flues embedded in the walls, venting from holes near the eves. Such a system requires, as a bare minimum, a plentiful supply of wood, and servants or slaves who will tend constantly to the fire to ensure that it is of just the right size and intensity. Although we sometimes think of hypocausts as being a quintessential feature of Roman domestic architecture, the reality was that only public buildings and the homes of the very well-to-do could afford the luxury of central heating. We may see, in Illustration 44, part of the hypocaust system in the Billingsgate house. The floor of the house was perched on the piles of tiles which we can see in the photograph. It was the space between the floor and the ground which was heated by the hot air produced by the furnace.

The main fabric of the house at which we are looking was made up of blocks of Kentish ragstone, the same material which was used for the fort, amphitheatre and city wall. Again, this marks out the owner as being prosperous. The floors were composed of the same terracotta cubes that we have seen elsewhere. We know nothing at all about those

44. The hypocaust at the house near Billingsgate.

who had this house built except that, for the time, they enjoyed a good life. Nor is it known why the decision was made to build a bathhouse in the garden in front of the house. This was a major undertaking and would have been costly both to build and operate. It has been suggested that perhaps the house was turned at some stage into some kind of hotel and that this accounted for the provision of a bathhouse, which would have been very extravagant for a private family. The truth is, we simply do not know.

The final house at which we shall look is a little different from the other two. They were in what was Londinium at the time that they were built and lived in. The next place we shall visit is technically in London, at least it is in Greater London, but 2,000 years ago it would have been in the heart of the countryside. It is a villa and to reach it we need to take a railway train to Orpington. This can be done from the central London stations of Victoria, Charing Cross and Cannon Street. If one turns right on leaving Orpington Station, the building which houses the remains of the villa is only a hundred yards or so from the station. The opening hours for this site are variable and it is best to check before setting out.

As may be seen from Illustration 45, what is on view is unimpressive, consisting of foundations, low walls and the barely visible traces of a hypocaust. This house is much larger and grander than the other two at which we have looked. Only ten rooms are visible today, in the area which has been fully excavated, but at its height the house, which was greatly altered over the years, probably had at least twenty rooms.

Crofton Villa, which is what this house is known as today, was unearthed in 1926, when a driveway was being prepared for some council offices. It was built about 140 AD and continuously inhabited until about 400 AD, when the Roman occupation of Britain largely came to an end. It was really a farmhouse, at the centre of an estate which covered 500 acres or so. The family which lived here must have been very well to do, for they had a hypocaust which was connected to all the rooms in their home. This ran not just under the floors, but

45. Crofton Villa.

also through the walls too. The amount of work entailed in keeping the furnace for such an extensive system stoked and maintained would have been considerable.

Life in a villa such as this would have been very different, and usually more luxurious, than living in the city. For the wealthy, it would have been preferable for a number of reasons. Just as our mental image of the interior of a Roman home is often misleading, so too are our ideas about what would lie outside the typical house in a Roman city like Londinium. We perhaps visualize sterile white streets, with classical columns and red roofs. Very seldom do we ever stop to ask ourselves what it might have smelled like.

There was no proper sanitation in Londinium. This meant that the bodily waste of over 30,000 people would need each day to be disposed of on an *ad hoc* basis. In most cases, this meant excrement being thrown out of the house and left in the near vicinity of other homes, which is not something about which we often think when looking at pictures of Roman cities. Of course, there were public latrines at the baths, but the citizens of Londinium could hardly be expected to trek to such a place every time they wished to open their bowels. Instead, they would use a pottery container and then dispose of the contents as best they could. Some had gardens upon which they could throw it, then too the street often had a central channel running down it which might get washed clean by the rain. Otherwise, it might simply be dumped behind the house. It is impossible to imagine how ghastly this would have made the nearby streets smell.

For those living in a villa, the case would be altered and the situation infinitely more pleasant. There would be a cesspit, sometimes more than one, into which the contents of chamber pots could be thrown by the servants. These would be some considerable distance from the house. All that was needed was a deep shaft, which might be covered with a removable lid to prevent the stink escaping too freely. When a cesspit was full, then the contents could be dug into the fields of the estate, just as today we sometimes use animal manure.

With a large estate surrounding it, the typical villa would have clean paths and plenty of privacy. Crofton Villa was at the centre of an estate with an area of about 500 acres. This is hard to visualize, but for those in London, 500 acres is a greater area than Hyde Park, Green Park and St James' Park all put together. There would have been plenty of room for leisure and recreation. Those living in places like this would have been like the gentleman-farmers of Victorian Britain.

The villa here was first built in about 140 AD and extensively altered over the next 260 years. It was not abandoned until about 400 AD. It is sometimes suggested that the traditional Roman way of life continued on estates like this for longer than it did in the cities. Cities of course have an infrastructure which must be maintained and if it is neglected, then things are apt to deteriorate fairly rapidly. This is not the case with a large farmhouse, which is what Crofton Villa was essentially. Even if trade with mainland Europe was hampered by the activities of the Saxon pirates who made such a nuisance of themselves in the late fourth century, this might only mean that those living here could be compelled to go without figs and wine. Enough crops would probably have been growing on the estate to make the place self-sufficient in wheat and other cereals. Add to this the livestock and poultry, and it would probably be possible to maintain a 'Roman' lifestyle in a way which could not have been done in London itself.

We have looked a little at the domestic life of people living in and around Londinium, but what did they do to amuse themselves? After all, there is more to life than simply having enough to eat and drink, and a warm bed to lie in at night. In the next chapter, we will look at two pastimes of Roman Londoners which were of great importance to them and of which evidence still exists in London that we may visit.

Chapter 10

Roman Londoners at Leisure

Human nature probably has not changed to any great extent over the last couple of thousand years, but the customs and traditions followed in various countries have certainly undergone dramatic alterations. Even in our own lifetimes we can see this process at work in Britain. Well within living memory, men and women were being hanged in London and newspapers eagerly reported the matter. Even schoolchildren watched as the classroom clock neared that fatal hour of nine, when executions took place. Today, 60 years after the last such event in Britain, we regard such an interest in the deliberate killing of a human being as horribly tasteless and not something we wish to see in a civilized society. So it is that when looking at the pleasures of society in Roman London, we must be prepared for the possibility that these will shock or disturb our modern sensibilities. One example should be sufficient to make the point.

There is, in Britain today, no more private act than opening one's bowels. There are countries in the world of course where public defecation is an unremarkable event, but Britain is definitely not among them. Even husbands and wives seldom or never witness their partner in the course of this act. This seems so naturally right and proper to us, that we are scarcely able to conceive any other way of ordering our lives. How very different was the case in Londinium. For the Romans, whether in Rome or London, sitting on the lavatory was a social activity, a chance to chat with one's friends and exchange a bit of gossip. Even more revoltingly, at least to the *mores* of our own age, they shared the means by which they cleaned their backsides afterwards, handing to each other sticks with pieces of sponge attached to the end!

This is one way in which the society of London 2,000 years ago seems quite alien to us today. It is as nothing though, when compared with what passed in those days for public entertainment.

In 1988, excavations were taking place beneath a building on the edge of Guildhall Yard in the City of London. The Guildhall is the City of London's municipal headquarters, analogous to a town hall, and the present building has stood near Guildhall Yard since the middle of the fifteenth century. It was not the first on the site though and there is reason to suppose that there was an important meeting place in this area at the time that the Anglo-Saxons first settled in London, a point to which we shall return. Not far from the Guildhall, and also on the perimeter of the large open space known as Guildhall Yard, was a Victorian art gallery which was destroyed during the Blitz in the early 1940s. In 1985, it was decided to rebuild this art gallery and for this reason, a deep basement was dug for the new building. It was during this process that an astonishing discovery was made.

For more than a century, archaeologists have been trying to track down the site of London's amphitheatre. It was a racing certainty that Londinium had had an amphitheatre, most important Roman cities having such a place. These were large, elliptical arenas, rather like present-day sports stadia, where crowds gathered to watch all kinds of things, from gladiatorial combat and executions to bear-baiting and displays of acrobatics. From time to time, tantalizing clues were unearthed which provided confirmatory evidence that there had once been an amphitheatre in the capital. An iron trident was dug up in Southwark, the kind of spear used by a type of gladiator known as a *retiarius*. The middle tine of this was bent, most likely by being used for fighting. This may be seen in Illustration 46. Then too, something which can only be described as a leather bikini bottom was found in Shadwell. This was the kind of costume worn by young girls who performed as acrobats in the amphitheatre, warm-up acts before the main event.

Amphitheatres were almost invariably situated outside and a little distance from city limits. This known fact acted, perhaps subliminally,

46. A trident used by a gladiator.

to misdirect those searching for Londinium's amphitheatre. The line taken by the Roman city walls was very familiar to archaeologists and so, at the back of their minds, was the idea that the site for which they were searching would have been beyond these walls. The truth was that the walls were built *after* the amphitheatre and so, unusually, Londinium's amphitheatre was to be found within them.

It was in February 1988 that ancient stone walls were found beneath the old art gallery. Archaeologists soon identified the masonry as Roman. The interesting thing was that the walls were curved. At first, it was speculated that these might have been part of a temple, but calculations of the area which the walls would have enclosed soon scotched that idea. Measurements revealed that the walls belonged to a structure which would have formed an ellipse which was 345ft long. Here at one time was an amphitheatre that could accommodate between 7,000 and 10,500 spectators, at a time when the total population of London did not exceed 30,000. This meant that the capacity of the amphitheatre was greater than that of a present-day venue in London like the Albert Hall.

Two features of London's amphitheatre had helped it to evade notice for so many years. One was that it lay within the walls of the Roman city, and the other unusual aspect is that it is almost adjacent to the fort at which we looked in Chapter 7. Again, this is very rare, but can also be explained by the fact that the amphitheatre was here *before* the fort, just as it was before the building of the city walls. Whatever the reason, it was clear that those seeking traces of London's amphitheatre had been looking in the wrong places all along.

The discovery of London's amphitheatre was the most significant archaeological event in the capital since the Temple of Mithras had been found in 1954. It was obvious to everybody that it would have to be preserved *in situ*, but this presented those building the new art gallery with something of a difficulty. The plans to which they were working called for two basements to the building, one of which would be below the level of the newly unearthed remains. Clearly, something quite out of the ordinary would be needed if the remains were both to be preserved where they were and a basement excavated beneath them. The solution was brilliant, involving an amazing feat of engineering. The lower basement was indeed excavated beneath the amphitheatre, but without causing it any harm or moving it from where it had been found.

To protect this most important archaeological site, a novel method of building was adopted. The usual procedure for large structures like office buildings or art galleries is to sink concrete piles all over the place as foundations upon which the weight will rest. Had this method been used for the new art gallery, then the newly-discovered amphitheatre would have been punctured in a dozen places and concrete pillars would have risen through the remains which had lain undisturbed for some 1,500 years. This would have been unthinkable for an archaeological site of such significance. It was a neat conundrum. How could the amphitheatre be preserved, while at the same time another basement was dug beneath it and a large building erected above it? The solution was on ingenious one. Instead of concrete piles, the weight of the building would be supported on a steel skeleton which rose from the sides of the building site, rather than in the middle as is more traditional. The walls, drains and surface of the amphitheatre were supported by a vast steel cradle, which transferred the weight to the sides of the building and enabled the builders to delve beneath for the vital new space which would be used to store precious documents safely.

It is time to go and examine this extraordinary location. London's Liverpool Street Station makes a good starting point, for it is served by three Tube lines as well as many railway lines from East Anglia and various suburbs. Before leaving the station, it must be mentioned that it is built on the banks of the River Walbrook, although no trace of the river is visible today. During building works here in the 1980s and 1990s, fifty skulls came to light, which were dated by means of radiocarbon testing to the time of the Roman occupation. We shall return to this point shortly, because it is relevant to our visit to the amphitheatre.

On leaving Liverpool Street Tube station, walk along Liverpool Street until you reach Blomfield Street. Turn left and carry on until you reach London Wall. Then turn right and cross the road. Walking along London Wall, we reflect that we are now crossing the valley of the Walbrook, whose route we followed down to the Thames in Chapter 1. We are now walking at a right-angle to the river, as though we were fording it. There is an archaeological puzzle associated with the Walbrook and this relates to the great number of skulls which have been found in it, all of them seemingly dating from the years of the Roman city. There are some very old legends which suggest that Boudicca's destruction of the first incarnation of Londinium was accompanied by the large-scale decapitation of prisoners, whose heads were thrown into the nearby river as a sacrifice, part perhaps of some religious ceremony. A more down-to-earth explanation has been offered, which is that floods might have washed human remains from burial grounds into the Walbrook, but there is a problem here. No other bones seemed to have been swept into the river in this way, only skulls. This sounds unlikely.

In the 1980s, at about the same time that the amphitheatre which we are on the way to visit was first uncovered, a grisly discovery was made when digging the foundations for a bookshop at 54 London Wall, which we find on our left as we walk along the street. These skulls have been supposed by some to be connected with the amphitheatre. A total of thirty-nine skulls were dug up during the redevelopment of this part of London Wall. Finding them in the valley of the Walbrook of course reminded archaeologists of all those other skulls found in that part of the City. During building work at Liverpool Street Station, another fifty skulls were found. All were dated to the centuries when the Romans lived in this part of London.

The most noticeable feature about the skulls found along the Walbrook in the 1980s is that they most of them show signs of having been severed while the victims were alive. These are definitely not the detritus from some long-forgotten flooding of a Roman burial ground; these people met violent ends and their heads were deliberately placed in or on the banks of the Walbrook. The skulls had various injuries, some of which had healed, such as what is known technically as 'blunt force trauma', which is to say heavy blows to the head, powerful enough to fracture the bones. There were also missing teeth and other injuries. The vertebrae showed signs of having been hacked through by sharp weapons such as swords or axes.

Of course, all this might well tend to confirm the old stories about such skulls belonging to the victims of some massacre which took place in Londinium during the Boudiccan revolt, except for one feature which made this almost inconceivably unlikely. This is that almost without exception, the owners of these remains had been young men aged between 18 and 35 years of age. We know from accounts of the event by Roman historians that all the able-bodied men who were able to move swiftly had abandoned Londinium before it was sacked by Boudicca and her forces. Those killed during the sacking of the city would have been the old people, women and children, not vigorous young men.

The most plausible explanation for the skulls is that they are the remains of gladiators from the nearby amphitheatre. This would account for the age and sex of the remains and also explain why so many had suffered injuries during life. Then too, the losers in gladiatorial combats, assuming that they had not been killed, were sometimes subject to the will of the crowd as to whether their lives were spared or they were swiftly dispatched. If a man had fought well, the crowd might indicate this by crying for mercy for him and, conversely, a cowardly and feeble gladiator might find the crowd booing and calling for his death. The bodies of those killed in this way might not be interred in the respectable burial grounds used by decent citizens, which were outside the city walls. Another possibility might be that these were criminals who had been executed, but this too would have been a public event in the amphitheatre and so either way, the skulls found here most probably belonged to those who lost their lives there.

Carry on walking along London Wall, crossing over the busy road of Moorgate and then watching out on the left for a footpath which leads to Coleman Street. Take this turning and then turn right onto Basinghall Avenue. The next turning on the left is Basinghall Street and we head south along this street. Walk down Basinghall Street and you will find yourself passing an impressive old building on your right. This is part of the Guildhall. After a while, you will come to a pedestrian passage on the right, blocked with steel bollards. Walk along this until you come to a large open space. This is Guildhall

Yard and it is a perfect instance of a concept at which we have already looked, that is to say what has been described as the persistence of memory in the city streets of this area of central London. For at least a thousand years, and almost certainly for twice that time, the space in front of you has been empty of buildings. We know this because we can see some medieval streets which deliberately avoided impinging upon what is now Guildhall Yard. Basinghall Street, along which we have just walked, is one of these. Like Aldermanbury, which runs along the other side of the Guildhall and Guildhall Yard, both streets curve to one side to avoid this space in which we are now standing. We saw something similar in Fenchurch Street, which we visited in Chapter 2, which swerves to one side to avoid the site of the forum which once stood where Leadenhall Market is today. This might be because some old taboo was felt about infringing upon the ruins of the ancients who had once lived in London, but there might be a more practical reason for avoiding the Roman remains. When the Romans put down foundations and erected walls, they were meant to last. In a previous chapter, it was mentioned that when the foundations for Goldsmiths' Hall were being dug, Roman foundations were encountered which were so solid that gunpowder had to be used to break them up. For the Anglo-Saxons, it would have been easier merely to skirt around ruins of that kind.

Standing now in Guildhall Yard, it will be observed that a broad black stripe runs in a curved line around the paved surface. This line marks the limits of the arena which once lay 20ft below the ground upon which we are standing. This gives some idea of the size of the thing. It may sheer coincidence that 2,000 years later this is still an open space, but on the other hand, it may not. If we walk forward a little, we shall find ourselves approaching a church on our left-hand side. This is St Lawrence Jewry, so called because of the number of Jews who once lived in this area until their expulsion in the thirteenth century. We notice that the church is set at an angle to the Guildhall. This is also odd, because this position of the church corresponds exactly to the great southern entrance to the arena of the amphitheatre. It is likely that the original medieval church was sited where Wren built its successor because it was intentionally placed to one side of the entrance.

Turning now to face the Guildhall itself, which is on the opposite side of the Guildhall Yard from the gap at which we have just looked, we remember that this is the oldest secular building in the whole of the City of London. It was built in the early fifteenth century, where an earlier Guildhall once stood. But why was this location thought an appropriate one for the centre of municipal government for the City? This too may be yet another way in which the memory of Roman London has been preserved down to the present day. One suggestion which has been made is that once the Anglo-Saxons began building their small wattle-and-daub homes among the ruins of the Roman city, that the amphitheatre would have been left as an open space and building would take place naturally around the walls, accounting for the way in which Basinghall Street and Aldermanbury swerve around an invisible curve. The arena might have been seen as the perfect place for outdoor meetings, somewhere for people to gather and express their opinions. We have something very similar today in Trafalgar Square, where vociferous people have for almost 200 years addressed meetings and crowds. This might have given the area around the arena a certain status as a debating platform and made it an obvious choice when the Saxons decided to build a meeting hall, which in time became the Guildhall. One last point is that the north part of the arena, where the Guildhall was built, was where the most important dignitaries were seated when the arena was functioning, something like the royal box in a modern theatre. Could this too be some folk memory and be the reason that the Guildhall stands today on that part of the old amphitheatre, rather than to the south, east or west?

To see what is left of the amphitheatre, we will need to go to the Guildhall Art Gallery, which is the unmistakeably modern-looking building which stands at right-angles to the Guildhall itself. Entry is free and once you are in the art gallery, there are plenty of signs pointing the way. It is of course necessary to descend into the earth, until we reach what was once the street level. Although the actual remains are sparse enough, they have a certain grandeur about them.

Steps lead down to what was once a passageway leading into the arena. This is the way that acrobats, gladiators and condemned criminals would have made their way. The audience would be seated high above this narrow corridor, which would at that time have had high walls on either side. It will be observed that a wooden drain runs the length of this passage and we shall have more to say about that in due course.

As we walk towards the arena itself, which lies ahead of us, we can see on either side, just before we get to the curved walls which surrounded the arena and protected the spectators from danger, two small cells or rooms on either side. It is supposed that these were waiting rooms, probably where animals were kept cooped up before they were released to face whatever fate had been decreed for them. There are grooves in the stone threshold of one of these cells, into which a vertically-rising wooden trapdoor, which could be raised from outside, would have fitted. Such a design would have prevented any animals, or for that matter people, trapped within from leaving until those organizing the games wished them to. On the left, it will be seen that a beam of wood lies across the threshold of one of the doors. Quite a lot of wood was recovered during the excavations here. Illustration 47 shows one of those holding cells with a piece of the original timber laying at the entrance to it. The ground was wet because of the presence of underground springs and so this prevented the air from reaching organic material and the process of decay starting. This is the same reason that the wooden drain which we can still see has also been preserved intact for almost 2,000 years.

We should be very grateful that the land around here is so waterlogged and that it preserved so much wood, because this has enabled archaeologists to calculate the age of the amphitheatre precisely

47. Part of the London amphitheatre, with original wood.

and also to tell us for how long it remained in use. This information has been provided by a technique known as dendrochronology, which perhaps needs a few words of explanation.

As we all know, trees grow a new layer each year and if we chop one down, then we can tell by counting the number of rings exactly how old the tree was. Of course, there is some slight variation in the size of the rings, depending upon climatic conditions and because of this it has been possible to match together the growth rings for trees over the years. A record has thus been built up of tree rings going back an astonishing 13,000 years. This means that by examining a wooden beam from a building or archaeological site, it is possible to tell to the very year when the tree from which it was cut was felled. To give an example of the precision with which this may be done, we need only consider the case of a house in the American state of Massachusetts. There had for many years been a claim that this house,

Fairbanks in Dedham, was the oldest wooden-framed house in the United States and that it had been built in 1640. Dendrochronological analysis of cores of wood taken from a beam in the house confirmed that it was from an oak tree which had been felled in 1638. A sample from another part of the house was from a tree which had been cut down in 1641. Wood at that time was not seasoned before use and so it was certain that the house had indeed been built between 1638 and 1641. The same techniques were used to study wood found during the investigation of the site of the London amphitheatre.

The wooden drain, which we can see beneath the glass windows set into the floor of the entrance passage along which we have walked, showed that the first incarnation of the amphitheatre, which was constructed from wood, was erected in about 72 AD. This is not all that can be gleaned from a close study of the timbers though, because the drain was repaired over the years, by the addition of other pieces of wood. These repairs took place over the course of the next 250 years, in other words into the fourth century AD. It is then a reasonable assumption that when people stopped maintaining the drains the amphitheatre had fallen into disuse. In short, we know that it was hosting entertainment between 72 AD and roughly 350 AD.

Once we walk into the small open space of what would have been the arena, we can see that the walls in front of us are gently curved. It will be recalled that it was this feature which first alerted archaeologists to the fact that they were dealing with an unusual building here. If we walk up the edge of the walls, without of course touching anything, it will be seen that sand and gravel lies at the foot of the walls. This is, incredibly enough, the original surface of the arena which has been dried and replaced here. This actual sand was used to absorb the blood from the exhibitions staged here.

The first incarnation of Londinium's amphitheatre was built on this site in about 72 AD. Originally, the amphitheatre was made up of earth banks covered with wooden seating and a stout wooden fence around the arena to keep in any animals and prevent prisoners about to be executed from attempting to escape. After 50 years or so, the wooden walls were replaced with the ones which can be seen today, the same solid and substantial masonry which may be seen in other Roman buildings in London. The walls are mere stubs today, because over the centuries they were broken down and looted for stones to use as building materials. In the last chapter, we visited the church of All Hallows by the Tower and saw how this worked in practice. The thick walls and arch of the Saxon part of the church are composed of stones and tiles taken from tumbled-down Roman buildings.

We must pause for a moment here and mention that our visual images of life in a Roman city often entail us imagining gleaming white buildings and statues. This was not at all the case, because of course the Romans were every bit as fond as modern people of seeing colourful surroundings. Their statues were not bright white. Close examination reveals traces of colour; these things were more meant to be realistic images and they were brightly painted, with the flesh also rendered realistically. In the same way, all those dull-looking inscriptions really had lettering picked out in red paint. The same applied to both private homes and public buildings such as the amphitheatre.

During the excavations on this site, fragments of purple and green marble were uncovered, which had obviously been cut into thin pieces for the purpose of decorating walls. This marble had been imported from Egypt and Greece and would have made a striking effect when inlaid as part of a pattern covering walls. Plaster and small pieces of wall paintings were also recovered. Far from being a sterile, white or grey building, the amphitheatre would have been a riot of colour. The walls, at least those visible to the public, would have been carefully plastered over and then painted with various motifs. Patterns would have been painted and also inlaid with marble. It really would have been quite a sight. The best modern comparison which we can make is probably the cinemas which were built in Britain in the years between the two World Wars. These were designed to look like elaborate palaces or fantastic, fairy-tale creations. Those living drab lives during the Great Depression in the 1930s would have been able, at least for a while, to forget their poverty and feel themselves being entertained in rich surroundings. So too with London's amphitheatre. Even apart from the displays themselves, the audience would be able to revel in the novel sensation of being in opulent and grand surroundings. It is accordingly difficult for us today correctly to visualize what a day at the amphitheatre would have looked like in London at that time.

A considerable amount of stonework remains; certainly enough to give a good impression of the size and sturdiness of the original structure. Although they are low today, none reaching more than 4 or 5ft in height, the masonry is massive and secure. The Romans built to last. It might be helpful at this point to reflect upon the strange nature of the entertainment provided in such places as this, for it runs counter to all modern ideas about how one might wish to relax on an afternoon off work.

Well within living memory in Britain, men and women were executed for murder. This was only ever seen as a grim necessity and the whole thing was done as quietly and neatly as could possibly be managed, in private, behind closed doors. In much the same way, the killing of animals is today a discrete business, concealed from the sight of the general public. We find it faintly appalling to think that during the Roman occupation, watching the death of both animals and humans was a hugely popular pastime for most people. We remember that the capacity of the amphitheatre might have been as great as 10,500 people, at time when the entire city contained no more than two or three times that number of inhabitants. There was room at these gory spectacles for half the people in Londinium to attend. This is because the space allocated to each person on the benches which surrounded arenas such as this was just 12in, a good deal less than most of us would expect these days if going to the cinema or theatre.

Before we become too smug and self-righteous about the superiority of our own moral standards in the things we like to watch as public displays, it is of course worth bearing in mind that both public executions and the bloody death of animals were universally regarded as making for a fine day out as late as the nineteenth century in this country. Extra railway trains were laid on to towns where a public hanging was to take place in the 1860s and the whole event was treated like a carnival. Bull-baiting, where a bull was pitted against ferocious dogs to see how long it would take before it was killed, was popular in the nineteenth century, as was cockfighting. Human nature does not change all that much over the centuries and the Roman enjoyment of the sight of death, although sublimated today into more acceptable forms, is still going strong.

The sequence of events in an arena such as that in London followed a fairly standard format. In the morning, animals, and sometimes the odd person too, were killed. Some of this part of the entertainment would be very similar to modern Spanish bullfighting, with various animals pitted against human hunters. Of course, the humans usually got the better in the match, but not always. To show off, some men would enter the arena almost naked, other than with a short sword, so demonstrating their courage. In Rome, men sometimes fought the beasts while they walked around the arena wearing stilts, to show their skill at the hunt. Sometimes, this ended badly for the show-off. Setting one fierce animal against another was also popular. A bear might be matched against a bull, for example. We can make a few shrewd guesses about this kind of thing, partly by looking at what happened in other amphitheatres, such as the Colosseum in Rome, which we know about through written accounts, and also by examining closely the debris found at the London arena.

The evidence for what actually took place at the amphitheatre here is both negative and positive. By negative, we mean that in the absence information to the contrary, then we assume that this amphitheatre was nothing remarkable or out of the ordinary and so much the same kind of things went on here, in pretty much the same order, as elsewhere. Then too, there is positive evidence, such as the leg bone of a European bear, which tells us pretty much for certain that animal fights took place here. Then too, there are the fragments of decorated pottery which have been found here. A large number of them show scenes from the games, either gladiatorial combat or animals being tormented or killed. It is a fair guess that these were by way of being souvenirs of the games.

After the animals had been killed, there were usually executions at around lunchtime. The methods used to put people to death varied and we do not know what they might have been in London. Sometimes, the condemned men were burned alive, at others they could be stabbed or beheaded. There are cases of animals being used in executions, so that a man would be put into the arena with a hungry leopard or lion. The whole idea was to make the death as amusing and entertaining as possible. Acrobats would sometimes give displays, if there were no victims to be put to death.

As far as the executions in London are concerned, it is possible that the skulls mentioned earlier, which were found during building work on London Wall, rather than belonging to gladiators, were the mortal remains of men who had been executed. Because it is almost only ever skulls which have been found in and around the course of the Walbrook, it is impossible to say what other injuries these people suffered, but there is no doubt that they all died as a direct consequence of head injuries. Their teeth were smashed, jaws broken, skulls fractured and vertebrae severed. It is possible that these lethal wounds were received while fighting to the death, but the other possibility is that these were condemned men who had been taken to the arena to be publicly executed. This is what the senior curator of archaeology at the Museum of London believes. She thinks that these young men were held at the fort, which was very close to the amphitheatre, and then then marched there to be killed by being decapitated in front of the crowds.

This might account for the clumsy way that some of these men had been despatched. In some arenas, soldiers competed to see which of them could take off a prisoner's head with just a single stroke of their sword. This was no easy feat and required the condemned man to remain absolutely still. There are hideous accounts of the crowd at such executions shouting warnings to the wretched man awaiting his death, so that he would flinch or even duck as the sword descended. This would mean that the blow would go awry and rather than a clean death, the victim would end up being hacked to death. A scenario of this kind would account neatly for the multiple injuries suffered by some of those whose skulls have been found.

At intervals between animal hunts, executions and gladiatorial combat, there would be novelty acts such as acrobats, clowns or performing animals. In this way, we can perhaps see the origins of the programme to which traditional circuses in this country adhered until the 1960s.

It was in the afternoon that the real events would begin, with gladiatorial combat. The sight of two armed men fighting each other to the death was an endlessly appealing one for the Romans, which is why this sort of thing lasted for centuries. The poet Juvenal famously remarked at the end of the first century AD, that as long as the people were provided with bread and circuses, they would never revolt. There seems to be something in this. But whereas our idea of circuses involves exciting but harmless entertainment, for the Romans the crux of the matter, the very *raison d'etre* of the amphitheatre, was death. The citizens may well have enjoyed watching acrobats, jugglers, wrestlers and even clowns as part of the programme, but all this was no more than a prelude to the proper business; watching young men fight to the death.

The solid evidence for gladiatorial combat in the London amphitheatre is sparse. Neither helmets nor armour have been found and few other indications that gladiators were a feature of the games which people watched. This is not altogether surprising of course. There were hundreds of soldiers stationed in the nearby fort, but very little in the way of their armour has ever come to light either. Unless we are fortunate enough to come across a city which has been frozen in time, like Pompeii or nearby Herculaneum, then most of the personal effects of those who lived and died there will long ago have been lost. The examples which we have of Celtic helmets and shields are ones which were deliberately flung into the Thames, probably as sacrificial gifts to the gods. The rest of the helmets would have been recycled for other purposes when they reached the end of their useful life. Bronze was a valuable substance and even if a sword, helmet or shield were to be damaged, it would not be simply thrown away.

One of the most entertaining aspects of gladiatorial combat lay in the different weapons with which the fighters were equipped, which meant that the two men battling it out needed to rely upon very different tactics if they hoped to defeat their opponent. One type of gladiator was the *retiarius*. This man wore almost no armour and was equipped with a weighted net, a long trident and a dagger. When pitted against a heavily-armed man, one wearing armour, then the only hope for the *retiarius* lay in dodging around and taking evasive action. His intention was to be able to throw his net over the head of the other man and then stab him while he was entangled in the net. If he was unfortunate enough to lose his net, then there was little hope for such a fighter.

Because of the way that they fought, running from their enemy and trying to attack from behind, there was a lot of prejudice against the *retiarius* among aficionados of the games. A number of Roman writers expressed the view that such men were not as manly and courageous as the fighters wearing armour. It was thought that the greater the area of bare skin which was exposed, the less manly was the figure which was cut.

It was noted above that little solid evidence has been found for the existence of gladiators in Roman London, but it was thought 25 years ago that not only had a gladiator been discovered, but a female one at that. This extraordinary piece of evidence about the possible existence of gladiators in Londinium came from south of the river, at the cemetery in Southwark. Although there has since been considerable scepticism, at the time that the discovery was announced by the Museum of London in 2000, it was presented as very strong evidence for not only gladiators in London, but female ones.

In 1996, archaeologists were working in Great Dover Street, which formed part of Watling Street in Roman times, the road which led from Kent to Londinium. While examining the graves of those buried beside the road, one in particular caught their attention. It was set a little way away from the walled part of the cemetery, which sometimes indicated that the dead person had lived in violation of the accepted social *mores* of the time.

The person in question had been cremated, but in rather a strange way. A wooden platform had been erected, with a pit below it, in which a fire was kindled. As the blaze consumed the wooden frame upon which the body was laid, so it gradually collapsed and the corpse was pitched into the fire. This is not a very efficient way of cremating a body and it is how archaeologists were able in the late twentieth century to deduce that the person in the grave was a woman; a small piece of the pelvis had remained uncharred, and this enabled them to determine the gender.

The funeral ceremony had been a fairly elaborate one, because it was possible by analysing the remains to see what the guests had been eating. The meal had included a dove and at least four chickens. In addition to that, figs, almonds and dates had also been on offer. This was quite a spread and it suggested that the woman had been somebody of significance. The grave goods which were buried with her offered a clue as to the woman's identity and position in life, or so it was claimed at the time of their discovery. There were burners for incense and also some ceramic lamps, brand new and never used. One of these had a representation of Anubis, the jackal-headed Egyptian god, on it, while the other had an image of a fallen gladiator. One explanation might be that she was a follower of the Egyptian religion which worshipped Isis. We know that there was such a temple in Southwark, because of a flagon found which had the name of this temple scratched upon it. Followers of this faith had a reverence for gladiators as symbolizing the very best ideals of Roman civilization. There was one more clue, which was that cones from the Stone Pine had been burned during the funeral. The significance of this is that such cones were often burned during gladiatorial games, to freshen the air between bouts and mask the smell of shed blood.

Some of the archaeologists who examined the remains of the woman and the grave goods concluded that she had in fact been a female gladiator. There had, during the late days of the Republic and the early centuries of the Empire, been a phase when women fighting to the death in the arena were a way of reviving the jaded palates of those who had grown used to watching men kill each other. There was thought by many though to be something inelegant or distasteful about the sight of women killing each other and the practice was officially banned about 200 AD.

The advocates for the theory that a female gladiator had been found in Southwark claimed that they believed that there was a 70 per cent chance that this was the correct explanation for all the various clues which had cropped up, but others were not so sure. The general consensus today is that the evidence is not strong enough to support such an idea, but for a time, the notion of a woman fighting in London's recently discovered amphitheatre captured the imagination of the British public.

At the beginning of this chapter, it was remarked that the Romans saw nothing strange about sharing communal lavatories, in which one might be seated next to a complete stranger. To those living in modern Britain, this sounds bizarre to the point of perversity. Another very private activity these days is of course having a bath, and in most homes even family members routinely close the door while they are in the bath. Again, this sounds to us today to be very natural and proper. Having a bath requires almost as much privacy as using the lavatory. It is worth remembering though that well within living memory in

Britain, many houses did not actually have bathrooms and that having a bath was a public, or at least semi-public, event. As late as 1950, fewer than half of British households had a bathroom, and well into the 1970s people were having to visit a public bathhouse if they wished to have a bath. This entailed queuing publicly at a special building and then sitting on a bench with others while waiting for a bath to become free. Having a bath was therefore a social activity, a chance to meet other people and perhaps chat with one's neighbours.

We remind ourselves about the situation relating to baths in Britain in the recent past, so that we can see that Roman Londoners were not so very different from us in their habits. Today, we might meet people and chat with them in a coffee shop or gymnasium, but for those living in Londinium, it was the public baths which were an important place to meet up with others.

In Chapter 3, we visited the site of the public baths at Huggin Hill, not far from St Paul's Cathedral. We return now to look at one of most popular leisure activities in Roman London; a visit to the baths. Following the instructions in Chapter 2 will bring us to the Cleary Garden, which is at the top of a fairly steep slope which leads down to the river. This spot was chosen for the bathhouse because of the topography. At the top of the hill several springs flowed down towards the Thames and this made it a perfect location for a bathhouse, because of course if there is one thing you want in a bathhouse, it is plenty of water. The proximity of the Thames was also handy, because it meant that waste water could simply run down naturally to the river, without anybody needing to worry about drainage.

At the top level of the Cleary Garden stood cisterns and tanks, fed by the streams flowing down from Ludgate Hill. These were thus filled naturally and whenever water was required, gravity did all the heavy lifting, as one might say, and all that was necessary was to open a valve and allow water from the tanks to run down into the baths themselves.

The bathhouse at Huggin Hill was built towards the end of the first century AD, probably about 80 AD. The city which had risen like a phoenix from the ashes of the Boudiccan destruction already had an amphitheatre and needed only a bathhouse to complete the image of the Roman idea of a civilized place to live. Because visiting the baths was more than merely a way to get clean, it was an event in itself, part of a cultured lifestyle. At the baths one could socialize, meet friends, exercise, gamble and gossip all in the same place. It was a peculiarly Roman practice and, for the Romans, a benchmark measure of civilization.

In Illustration 14 (see page 34), we see a reconstruction of the bathhouse which stood here. Because it was built into a hillside, many retaining walls and specially constructed foundations were necessary, to prevent the buildings slipping downhill and tumbling into the nearby river. In Chapter 3, we examined one such retaining wall, which even today is as sturdy as it was 2,000 years ago. If we walk down the steps into the Cleary Garden, we can visualize the scene when this was part of Londinium. The upper parts of the gardens would have consisted of water tanks and as we walk down, we come to the areas where the buildings themselves would once have stood. These extended to our left and right, as well as directly in front of us, because the bathhouse occupied perhaps 75 yards of the riverbank at this point.

When we reach the bottom of the gardens, we can see on the left the retaining wall which would once have supported some of the buildings. The main part of the complex, which consisted of seven separate rooms, lies in the basement of the office block we see ahead of us at the bottom of the slope. There is unfortunately no public access to the remains. We are able to visit the fairly well-preserved remnants of a private bathhouse of course, that attached to the house in Billingsgate which we looked at in the last chapter, and since the procedure for a small establishment like that was similar to the way that a large public bathhouse would have been used, we can refer to the place that we *can* visit and then scale up for thinking about the Huggin Hill baths.

Before discussing in detail what went on in a Roman bathhouse, we ought first to explain that what the Romans meant by 'baths' was very different from what we mean by the word today. Essentially, having a bath in modern London entails immersing oneself in warm water and using soap to clean the body. This sounds so obvious as to be hardly worth mentioning, but it was not at all the Roman idea of a bath. Cleansing was accomplished by sweating and the application of olive oil to the skin, rather than by scrubbing with soap and water. It is true that in most public baths there were facilities for covering oneself entirely with hot or cold water, but this was more for the pleasurable feeling or supposed benefits to health than as anything to do with becoming clean.

Before looking at what was on offer at the public bath in Huggin Hill, perhaps returning to the smaller and private bathhouse at Billingsgate which was described in the last chapter, might be helpful. The modest facilities there consisted of a *frigidarium*, or cold room, a *tepidarium*, or warm room, and finally the hottest of the rooms, the *caldarium*. These represent the basic sequence of the Roman bath, which had more in common with the Finnish sauna than with the modern British idea of a bath. The clothes were removed in the cold room, before moving to the warm room, to become acclimatized to a higher temperature. After that, it was time for the hot room, which would cause profuse sweating. Oil would be rubbed into the skin and then scraped off with an instrument known as a strigil. It was thought that dirt and impurities would be sweated out through the pores. This sequence would be repeated as often as desired.

The heat for the Roman baths was provided by hypocausts, which were a way of spreading hot air from a furnace throughout a room. Today, we rely upon hot water for our central heating, but the Romans used air. As we have already discussed, this was circulated under floors and through walls in the wealthier homes and was also the means by which the rooms were heated in the baths. There were, in the baths at Huggin Hill, pools of water in which it was possible to immerse oneself entirely. This was refreshing and in larger establishments these were the size of swimming pools and indeed, people did actually swim in them. Although the pools at Huggin Hill were of a more modest size, they still required to be filled with water and for the water to be changed regularly and it was for this reason that siting the baths on terraces beneath springs of water was perfect.

These public baths were used by all classes of society; rich and poor, men and women. The entrance price was modest enough to ensure that nobody was excluded by the cost. Apart from maintaining hygiene, they were a place to meet and chat with other people, to make business deals, play gambling games with dice and to undertake physical exercise. Most public baths had a courtyard where it was possible to lift weights or do some physical jerks. At some times in Roman history, men and women used the baths at different times of day, but there were also periods when it was the custom for men and women to take the baths together. There is no record as to what the attitude was in Londinium towards mixed bathing of this kind.

For reasons at which we can only guess, these particular baths were pulled down and demolished in around 200 AD. There were other changes afoot in the city at that time and it is possible that the expense of maintaining them became simply too great.

There was at least two other public bathhouses in Roman London, including one to be found where Cheapside is now. It was a smaller place than Huggin Hill and because of its proximity to the fort, it has been thought that perhaps this served only the needs of the soldiers stationed there. This is mere speculation though, as there is no evidence to support such an idea. There was also, as we saw in Chapter 4, a larger bathhouse in Southwark, which may well have been connected in some way with the army as well.

The distinction between public and private bathhouses may be a little misleading, because there was an overlap. Owners of domestic bathhouses would sometimes rent them out to people and even allow the general public to use them. They were expensive places to maintain and letting others use them for payment helped to defray the cost. Then too, it is not always possible to tell the difference, 2,000 years later, between a public and private bathhouse. Returning to the one at Billingsgate, we have good reason to suppose that the house existed without a bathhouse for 60 or 70 years. Why did the occupants suddenly decide to go to all the trouble and expense of building one? Of course, it could just have happened in the same way that the owner of a big house today will have a swimming pool installed in his home if he is wealthy enough. On the other hand, it might have been the case with Billingsgate that the private house was sold to somebody who wished to open it as a hotel or boarding house and felt that a bathhouse would make it a more desirable place to stay.

Visiting the bathhouse at Billingsgate brings home to us very clearly, exactly what it would have been like to use a Roman bath, because we can actually see the facilities in detail. Illustration 48 shows a reconstruction of what it would have looked like in use, with the roof cut away to allow us to peep inside. The first room which was entered, the cold room, was probably connected to the house by a covered passage. It was the largest room in the bathhouse and at one end had a large cistern full of cold water. The floor of this room may be seen in Illustration 49. Wooden sandals would have been provided here, because in the other two rooms the floor was hot. Quite a time would have been spent in the warm room and there were seats along the wall to sit down and relax. Then the users would move to the hot room and this would be very much like a Turkish bath or sauna. After building up a good sweat, the users would move back to the cold room and splash themselves with cold water. The cistern which contained this water may still be seen.

From all of this, it will be seen that even to use the same word, 'bath' to describe both what the Romans got up to in bathhouses and what we do in the privacy of the bathroom in our own home is confusing. These were actually two entirely different activities. For us in modern Britain, a bath is a solitary pleasure, with the chief aim

48. Billingsgate bathhouse at it would once have looked.

49. What remains of the bathhouse at Billingsgate.

being to remove dirt and sweat from the skin. However, the purpose is essentially functional. We talk of having a 'quick' bath or shower. For the Roman though, this was an activity in itself; the idea of having a quick bath would have been simply baffling. It was not something one might hurry through, so that one might then pursue one's social life; this *was* the social life. Hurrying a day at the baths for a Roman would have been as perverse as a modern woman trying to hurry through a spa day.

Chapter 11

Religion in Roman London

The subject of religion in Roman London was very often closely associated with cemeteries and the dead. Although they were deeply and inextricably linked together in Roman life, we shall treat of them in two separate chapters. We see an echo of this connection between religious buildings and cemeteries in our own time, with our places of worship being traditionally surrounded by the dead. Those who worship in churches today take this juxtaposition for granted and do not think twice about entering their church by walking past the interred bodies of those who have gone before. Churches and graveyards go together, as the old song has it, like a horse and carriage. However, I have decided to deal with these two matters separately.

The major religions in the modern world tend to be intolerant of rivals and to regard themselves as the only true path to salvation. The God of the Old Testament is famously jealous and insists in the Ten Commandants that his followers shall have no other gods beside him. Christianity, springing as it did from the Jewish faith, inherited a good deal of this belief that might be summed up as the feeling that if you adopted Christianity, then it followed as night follows day that all other religions must be false and lead people into error. We see much the same sentiments of course in Islam. The Romans though had a very different view of the case.

As most readers will be aware, the Romans worshipped a pantheon of gods and goddesses who were lifted wholesale from the belief-system of the ancient Greeks. They renamed them of course, so that the king of the gods, Zeus, became Jupiter, and Ares, the god of war, became Mars, but otherwise the deities of Greece and Rome are identical. For the Romans though, this did not mean that they wished to force their beliefs upon others, nor did they try to suppress the religious practices and beliefs of those territories which they conquered. The only time that they did this was when religion acted to oppose their rule. We remember the Jewish rebellion against Rome, which was at least as much a revolt against a heathen occupier as it was a national struggle. The druids' stronghold on the Isle of Anglesey, off the coast of Wales, was attacked and destroyed by a Roman army at the same time that Boudicca was sacking Londinium, but this was because the druids were inciting insurrection, rather than because they worshipped different gods.

Julius Caesar, in his writings on the subject of the Celts, suggests that they worshipped the same gods as Rome, but under different names. This, if so, would hardly be surprising. The Roman, Greek and Celtic cultures all had their roots in the Indo-European tradition. This ethnic group once lived in and around what is now Ukraine and perhaps 2,000–3,000 years before the Romans landed in Britain, the Indo-Europeans swept westwards and colonized most of Europe. They brought with them a religion which venerated the 'Sky Father', who in time became known to the Romans as Jupiter. It is entirely possible that when they landed in Britain, the Romans really *did* find the people there following a similar religious creed to that to which they themselves subscribed.

Whatever the reason, the Romans were happy to endorse, and even worship at, the sites which the Britons regarded as holy. More than that, they would build their own shrines at hilltops, springs and wells which were venerated by the Celts and so produced what we know today as Romano-Celtic temples. Before discussing one such, which we are able to visit, it might be helpful to discuss one or two other ways in which Roman religious practices and beliefs were similar to those which they encountered after invading Britain.

Religion, for both Britain and Rome, entailed contracts and bargains made between humans and the gods. There was little idea of virtue being its own reward, as we often think to be the case with Christianity. For the Romans and Britons both, it was very much a case of you scratch my back and I'll scratch yours. Sacrifices were made to the gods and gifts given to their temples, and in return the donors expected favours to be done for them. For instance, a captain might promise to renovate a temple, provided that the gods aided him in a coming battle. It was understood that the gods were as fickle and vain as mortals, and that they must be flattered, cajoled and bribed into being on the side of this person or that.

Some spectacular bronze swords, helmets and shields have been recovered from the River Thames and it is hypothesized that these were not lost in the water through some mishap, but rather were deliberately cast in as sacrifices. These items would have been as costly as a new sports car might be today and by casting them into the river publicly as an offering for the gods, some wealthy Celtic chieftain would demonstrate both his piety and his wealth. He would be assured of the gods' favour for a good long while.

All this was readily understood by the Romans when they settled in Britain, as was another aspect of Celtic religion; the idea that rivers, wells and other sources of water were sacred and that they formed a bridge between the realm of the gods, and of course the land of the dead, and this living world of ours. That Romans and Celts both shared this slightly odd belief almost certainly indicates that it had a common source in the ancient past of the Indo-Europeans, who were the ancestors of both peoples.

So it was that when the Roman invaders found a native British cult at the city which we now know as Bath, which centred around hot springs and was dedicated to a goddess known to the locals as Sulis, they embraced it enthusiastically, seeing in Sulis an incarnation of their own goddess Minerva. With no difficulty whatsoever, a temple developed at Bath which was dedicated to Sulis Minerva. This provides a perfect instance of what was seen in London in the early years of the Roman occupation. Sacred wells, springs or other locations were adopted without hesitation by the conquerors and turned into places of worship or cult sites where Britons and Romans could both practise their religion in harmony.

It was remarked in an earlier chapter that the earliest written references to Londoners was found in Southwark on a marble tablet. This mentions Mars Camulus. Camulus was a Celtic god whom the Romans regarded as being cognate with their own Mars, the god of war. He was evidently a popular deity in Britain, for the largest town in Britain, Camulodunum, modern-day Colchester, was named after this Camulus. So it was that once they had established themselves in London, the Romans simply accepted the existing holy sites and let it be known that these were also dedicated to their own gods.

Of course, later on the Christians played much the same game and took over sacred groves and wells, but they were a little more uncompromising and less willing to acknowledge any similarities between one religion and another. We have already visited two places in London where we might perhaps have seen this happening and can trace continuity of the religious significance of a site all the way from the Celts to the present day. Both of these places are now churches and both were founded on sites with holy wells.

The church of St Bride's in Fleet Street dates back at least to the sixth century AD. There is stonework remaining from that time in the crypt of the church. But there is also a Roman floor, made up of terracotta tesserae, so we may sure that the site has been built on for a couple of thousand years. Yet this place was almost certainly of significance before the Romans came, because there was a well here which was reputed to have holy properties. This is why the prison which once stood nearby was called Bridewell, a corruption of Bride's Well. On the other side of the river is Southwark Cathedral, which also dates back as far as the early Saxon period as a Christian site. In Chapter 4, we saw that there had been a well on this site at the time of the Roman occupation and that various religious articles, including the image of a Celtic god, had been deposited there.

It is time to look at what little remains of the only Romano–Celtic temple which can be visited in London. Earthworks marking the site of one such temple may be seen today in Greenwich Park. There is reason to think that the temple at Greenwich was built because two traditions happened to coincide at that location. On the one hand, there was the Roman acceptance and adoption of holy places which they found in the areas which they invaded and occupied, and on the other there is the fact that it was something of a custom to build temples and establish burial grounds by the roads leading into the city. Since the major road of Watling Street passed through what is now Greenwich Park, it would have been a natural place anyway for a temple to be set up. But then too, there is reason to suppose that this spot was somehow special, in a religious or superstitious sense, long before the arrival of the Romans.

Greenwich Park is most conveniently reached by the Docklands Light Railway. It is only a short walk from the station to the park. Simply walk up Croome Hill and then turn into a gate on the left which gives access to the park. You will observe that the area of grassland which lies beyond this gate is not flat, but is rather covered with circular mounds varying from 10 to 30ft in diameter. We are most of us aware that some parts of England, Salisbury Plain for instance, form part of an ancient ritual landscape, covered in burial mounds and monuments such as standing stones. Strange as it may seem, Greenwich Park is just such a landscape. The backdrop of the shining office buildings of Docklands which can be seen in the distance, make this see all the more incongruous. Illustration 22 (see page 66) shows the scene. The low saucer-like domes which you can see are burial mounds. Most are assumed to be Saxon, but others probably date from the Bronze Age. In other words, Greenwich Park was very likely a special place before the Romans came to this country. That many people were interred on the hilltop suggests that this area had some religious significance, just as Salisbury Plain did thousands of years ago. This may well explain why the Romans built a temple here.

50. Artist's impression of the Greenwich temple in 300 AD.

To reach the site of the temple we need to walk towards the observatory, the building right in front of us, and then carry on to the other side of the park. It is possible to distinguish the rectangular outline of the temple which once stood here. Illustration 50 shows us what this would have looked like when it was operating. It was a typical Romano-Celtic structure of the kind found all over the country. There is the temple itself and then a low wall surrounding what is regarded as the sanctified area which extends beyond the building. This is a little bit like the wall surrounding a church and burial ground, with the ground inside being in some way 'hallowed'. Illustration 51 shows part of the site today.

Watling Street, the major Roman Road which ran from Dover to London and from there on to Wales, passed only a few yards from this spot. This meant that travellers to London could not have failed to see the temple as they came within sight of the city. This is something which can be seen also at the temple complex in Southwark, which we visited in Chapter 4, where those entering London from the south or east encountered temples and tombs by the roadside. Those entering from the north would similarly have to pass through a burial ground

51. The site of the Greenwich temple today.

with prominent tombs roughly where Liverpool Street Station now stands. Illustration 3 (see page ix) shows some tombs which are still standing in Greater London. They too were by a road. Originally, they would have been covered with plaster and painted bright red, ensuring that nobody would be able to miss them. It is likely that the fields of tombs outside the gates of Londinium would have been similarly unmistakable.

Just to make this perfectly clear, entering Londinium from the south, via Watling Street from Dover or Stane Street from Chichester, would mean passing through burial grounds and a temple complex before reaching the city itself. Outside the city gates at Aldgate, Bishopsgate, Newgate and Ludgate too, were burial grounds with prominent tombs. Approaching the city from Dover would entail passing two burial grounds and three temples, the one in Greenwich and then the next two by the entrance to Londinium in Southwark.

The temple at which we are now looking was discovered in 1902 and at first, all that was certain was that this had been a Roman building. Gradually though, from the nature of articles found on the site, especially inscriptions, and also from the general layout, it became obvious that this was a typical Romano-Celtic temple. There was the central building, the *cella*, which was the holiest part of the place and as such forbidden to ordinary people, and the sacred enclosure, delineated by a wall. Entering this walled area was as close as anybody other than priests could get to the presence of the god or goddess. This is of course very different from the modern arrangement, where worship and prayer always take place indoors, within a special building. Some idea of how the place might have looked when it was functioning may be gleaned from looking at Illustration 50. This shows a reconstruction which was devised for a television programme about this temple.

Until a few years ago, there was at this site the most insignificant Roman structure ever seen. So small was it, that it was sometimes concealed if the grass has been allowed to become too shaggy and unkempt. This was a tiny section of tessellated flooring, of the kind at which we have looked both in St Bride's Church and Southwark Cathedral, although on a more modest scale. In fact, it looked for all the world like an old chimney-pot which has somehow fallen onto the grass. This, together with a few bumps and hollows in the ground, is all that can now be seen of the temple which stood here for centuries. Illustration 52 is of the mosaic flooring which is now the only surviving fragment of the building. It has now been removed, something which we shall discuss in a later chapter. The general layout has been worked out from what was found over the years and when the television programme *Time Team* sponsored an excavation here in 1999, they produced an image of what the temple might have looked like at its height. This is based upon all the available evidence found so far and may be seen in Illustration 50.

One thing which has been discovered about the temple at Greenwich is the extraordinary length of time that the place was in

52. The remains of the temple in Greenwich Park.

use; from at least 100 AD to about 400 AD, roughly the time when Britain ceased to be part of the Roman Empire. For a place of worship to have endured that long, we can probably assume that it was an important location. Perhaps the presence of the burial mounds had something to do with this. The site was not chosen at random, but like most Romano-Celtic temples was more likely established where some shrine, grove, well or other place sacred to the native inhabitants was already situated.

An example of the way in which Romans sometimes chose pre-existing places of religious importance to the Celtic inhabitants of Britain may be see just outside London, in the Essex town of Harlow. A Romano-Celtic temple was discovered there and because it was on open land and there was no mad rush to excavate it, as happens when building developers in London give a site over to archaeologists for a limited time, more has been learned about the relationship of the

Romano-Celtic temples with the previous practices in the country than in other places. The discoveries there might well have implications for the temple in Greenwich.

The temple in Harlow was established on the bank of a river, as often happened with such places, in this case the Stort. The Roman temple which was examined was nothing particularly special, it was what lay beneath it which was of great interest. There were many freshly-minted Roman coins, which had clearly been left as votive offerings. Underneath the remains of the Roman building though, was found an earlier, wooden structure. Beneath this were Iron Age coins, produced before the arrival of the Romans. It was obvious that long before the Romans came, a Celtic temple stood here, where worshippers followed much the same practices and traditions as the occupiers when they took over the site. The greatest surprise though came when archaeologists dug below the Celtic temple, because they came across urns filled with cremated human remains from the Bronze Age. Whatever was going on with the Romano-Celtic temple followed some religious ritual which predated the arrival of the Romans by over a thousand years. There was also the association between a temple and the burial of human remains, which was to be a recurring theme of the Roman occupation.

It is altogether possible, indeed likely, that the temple in Greenwich at which we are looking has a similar history. That it was built along the line of a chain of round barrows strongly suggests that this spot was somehow sacred to the people who lived round and about. More than 300 coins were found here, in precisely the same way that they were at the temple in Harlow. Pieces of plaster were found, with signs that there were columns around one of the buildings here, probably the *cella*, which were made of brick and then covered with plaster and painted to appear like marble.

A recurring theme of this book has been the continuity of memory in London; the way in which the prehistoric use of a site might be transformed into a place of significance to the Romans and then will linger on to the modern day. In Fleet Street, we saw how an ancient well became for some reason the focus of attention by the Romans and then later was transformed into a church, the design of which is known throughout the world for being the inspiration for the traditional wedding cake. We saw too how the open space of the arena at the amphitheatre has remained clear of buildings for thousands of years. Something very similar appears to have happened in part of Southwark in south London.

Readers might be familiar from Chaucer with the name of the inn from which many pilgrims set off to visit the shrine of Thomas á Becket at Canterbury. This was the Tabard and it stood at the point in Southwark where Watling Street and Stane Street met before reaching London Bridge. Those making this pilgrimage travelled east along Watling Street, passing the site of the Roman temple and prehistoric and Bronze Age burial mounds in Greenwich at which we looked earlier in this chapter. This gave the area around that part of Southwark a distinctly religious flavour in the Middle Ages. By curious coincidence, if indeed coincidence it is, a temple complex once occupied this part of London and the district where the Tabard Inn would one day be built, was, in essence, a religious district a thousand years earlier.

Visiting the area of the Romano–Celtic temples in present-day Southwark will lead us to a most surprising, one might even say astonishing, discovery. If we take a train to London Bridge Station, also on the London Underground system, and then walk south along Borough High Street, this will lead us to our destination. On our left, we pass Talbot Yard, which is where the Tabard Inn stood until its demolition in the nineteenth century. We carry on along Borough High Street for a short distance before reaching Tabard Square, a new development during the construction of which many archaeological discoveries were made.

In one of the shafts was found a marble tablet with an inscription, which had been inked in, in red. This read;

To the Divinities of the Emperors (and) to the god Mars Camulus. Tiberinius Celerianus, a citizen of the Bellovaci, moritix, of Londoners the first.

It is the first ever recorded reference to Londoners. It is a curious thing that those living north of the Thames are sometimes a little snobbish about south London and yet the earliest references to London and Londoners both come from south of the river. Even more curiously, both are made in connection with religion. The very earliest written evidence for the name of 'London' is to be found on a flagon from the first century AD, which was found near Tooley Street, not far from London Bridge. It bore the inscription, 'LONDINI AD FANVM ISIDIS'. This translates as, 'To London at the temple of Isis'. An altar from the temple of Isis, who was an Egyptian deity, was found across the river, having been used as part of the riverside wall.

There are, sad to say, no visible remains to be seen of the temples which once dominated this area. There is, however, one relic which may be seen today. It suggests to us that one of the temples which stood here was probably dedicated to Minerva, the Roman goddess of wisdom. We have reason to believe this because of a truly extraordinary survival which lies just a short walk from Tabard Square.

We leave Tabard Square and walk south to Great Dover Street. We are now leaving what might be not inaptly be termed the temple district and upon crossing Great Dover Street, find ourselves in an area which was a large Roman cemetery. This cemetery is bounded by Great Dover Street, Borough High Street and Harper Road. Many remains of burials and not a few funerary monuments have been unearthed in this part of Southwark. It is a district of particular interest because it contains one of the most extraordinary Roman remains in the whole of London. What is even more remarkable is that although it has been standing here, in plain sight, for centuries, not one person noticed it until the summer of 2021!

If, having crossed Great Dover Street, we walk down Globe Street and turn left, we shall find ourselves in Trinity Street. A short walk will bring us to Trinity Church Square on the left, which is centred around a garden which was laid out a decade or so before Queen Victoria ascended the throne.

The garden in front of the church was established in the 1820s by a local builder called William Chadwick. It is now a private square and usually open only to the residents of the surrounding houses, but it is not necessary to enter the garden to see what we have come to look at. Towering above the shrubbery is an enormous statue of a king, reputedly Alfred the Great. This statue is larger than life, about 8.5ft tall, and it has stood here for at least 200 years. A picture dated 1831 shows the church with the gardens in front of it and the statue in its present position. It may be seen in Illustration 1 (see page viii).

The statue of King Alfred in Southwark has long been recognized as the oldest outdoor statue in London and there have for many years been two chief theories about its origin. Since 1950 the statue in Trinity Church Square has been a Grade II listed monument and the listing for it at that time mentions two possible origins. To quote from the listing, which makes no mention of Alfred the Great and refers simply to 'statue in centre of Trinity Church Square':

> Statue of a king on a stone plinth, late C14 style. Erected in the square before 1836, resited. Limestone with upper part and most of sides and back restored in artificial (probably Coade) stone. Back of statue quite plain as though designed for a niche. Provenance uncertain but said to be one of 8 medieval statues from the north end towers of Richard II's Westminster Hall. Alternatively, could be one of a pair representing Alfred the Great and Edward the Black Prince, made for the garden of Carlton House in the C18.

From the very earliest time of its appearance in its present location, therefore, mystery had surrounded this statue. It will be observed from the listing that it was found to be of limestone, with some additions which were made of some kind of artificial stone. This hinted at an older statue which had been remodelled or altered in some way.

The local legend that the statue of Alfred the Great was very ancient, dating back perhaps to medieval times, is intriguing. We have explored the idea of what might be called the 'persistence of memory', whereby some exceedingly old part of London might leave an impression which lingers on to the present day. This phenomenon often seems to be connected with churches. We must remember that this church and the square with the statue in it lie a stone's throw from the temple complex which we walked through to get here, that is to say the Tabard Square area. We are standing here near the junction of two Roman roads, Watling Street and Stane Street, which happens to be the site of a Roman cemetery. A number of burials from that time have been investigated here and funerary monuments uncovered.

Because the statue of King Alfred is a listed monument, it must be kept in good condition and standing out in the open in all weathers for a couple of centuries had, by the summer of 2021, left it looking a little the worse for wear. It was accordingly decided that it was time to clean it up a little and repair any minor damage. Trinity House, the maritime charity who are the custodians of the statue, teamed up with the Heritage of London Trust and hired London Stone Conservation Ltd to undertake cleaning and also to carry out any necessary conservation work. This led to one of the most astounding archaeological discoveries made in London since the Temple of Mithras was unearthed in 1954.

As cleaning progressed, loose and crumbly material was removed from the surface of the statue, revealing in more detail just how it had been made. The lower half consisted of South Cotswold limestone, commonly known as Bath Stone. About 90 per cent of the Roman statues sculpted in this country are of Bath Stone. It is what is known technically as a 'freestone', which is to say that there is no grain or particular direction in which it must be cut. Onto the bottom part of this limestone statue, which was of a right leg draped in folds of cloth, had been grafted the body of the crowned king. This had been made of an artificial stone called Coade Stone. Once the two halves had been joined together, the whole thing was coated with a hard mortar, to conceal any sign of the joins. A word or two about Coade Stone might not come amiss.

In the late eighteenth century an enterprising woman called Eleanor Coade devised the artificial stone which bears her name. It was a ceramic made by grinding up silica, terracotta and various other materials, mixing it into a paste which could be pressed into a mould and then fired in a kiln for a very long time, four days or so. The resulting substance was enormously strong and very resistant to weathering and erosion. It was very useful for moulding statues, architectural details, garden ornaments and anything else. The best-known example of Coade Stone is the lion which stands at the north end of Westminster Bridge. Eleanor Coade kept her formula a closely-guarded secret and even today, there is uncertainty about its exact composition. What is certain is that it could be moulded like clay and fired in a kiln, later being chiselled and sanded as necessary.

It appeared that the statue of King Alfred was formed by taking the lower half of an existing statue and then moulding an upper half, which was somehow attached to the other part. Judicious filing and work with abrasives then removed all sign of any join and the whole thing was then coated thinly with mortar, so that it was impossible to distinguish one part from another. Despite the ingenuity displayed by those devising this curious work of art, the story of what had been done was preserved orally, passed down by word of mouth through the generations, until even a couple of hundred years later the rumour persisted that this was a statue with a strange history and had existed for hundreds of years before it was erected in the newly-created garden in Trinity Church Square as a representation of Alfred the Great.

It was during the restoration of this strange item that two archaeologists and a geologist looked with fresh eyes upon the lower half of King Alfred and made an astonishing discovery. They realized that all the indications were that this was a part of an enormous Roman statue of a goddess, which would at one time have stood 9ft high and probably been the central feature of a temple. Since it is known that there was a temple complex just 250 yards from where the statue now stands, it was almost certain that this is where the thing came from originally. The wonder of it was that nobody had put together the pieces of the puzzle before.

Looked at objectively, the lower part of the statue in Trinity Church Square has a decidedly feminine air about it, as can be seen from looking closely at the lower half of the statue, as it may be seen in Illustration 1 (see page viii). The folds of cloth and even the shapely leg look as though they belong to a woman, rather than a man. The style too is identical to that of other Roman statues depicting goddesses. It bears an uncanny resemblance to a statue of Minerva from Cambridgeshire. Professor Martin Hennig, a leading authority on Roman art, was called in to give an opinion on the statue and had no doubt at all what he was looking at. He believed it to have been originally a twice life-size cult statue, almost certainly of Minerva, one which would have stood in a niche in a temple. He was able to deduce this because the back is flat and lacks detail, suggesting strongly that this part of the statue was never intended to be seen.

We are looking therefore at the largest Roman statue ever found in Britain and one which has stood here, in full view, for 200 years. The question is though, for how long before that was it visible to any passer-by? It has been suggested that perhaps it had been buried nearby and dug up in the course of excavations for building houses or even when the garden where it stand was being laid out. That is certainly one possibility. Another is that it has been above ground since the Romans left Britain in the fifth century, perhaps used for another purpose during all those centuries. We are never likely to know the answer to this. It is, to say the least of it, very strange that there should be a memory handed down for so long that this statue was special, being of great antiquity. Whatever the explanation, it is now possible to view the largest and most complete Roman sculpture on public display in Britain.

There was perhaps something about the road leading from Kent to London which made it special from a religious point of view. This might be part of a tradition which existed even before the coming of the Romans in 43 AD, because although Romano-Celtic temples are found on the line of Watling Street, so too are burial mounds predating the Roman invasion. Apart from the ones at which we looked in Greenwich Park, there are many others which line what was once Watling Street.

Only one Roman temple still exists which may be visited and that lies on the banks of the Walbrook. The story behind this temple and its peregrinations around London is a fascinating one. As with the Cripplegate fort, the key figure behind the preservation of this important piece of London's history is W.F. Grimes, who was in the 1940s and 1950s the director of the Museum of London. Once again, we have the Blitz to thank for the discovery, for it was while the remains of various bombed buildings were being cleared away in the area along the Walbrook valley in 1954 that some strange ruins were found beneath the foundations of the buildings which were being demolished. That they were Roman was obvious, but what was not so plain was the nature of the building itself. It was not until the very last day of the archaeological dig that the mystery was solved, for it was on that day, Saturday, 18 September 1954, that the statue of a man wearing a Phrygian cap was dug out and Grimes at once recognized the figure as Mithras. He knew then that this was a Mithraeum, a place of worship for the followers of the Persian religion of Mithraism.

Something about the finding of this Roman temple appealed to the people of London and they flocked in their thousands to see it. Huge queues formed, as ordinary Londoners of all ages and classes filed past the ruins to look at what they were assured was a major discovery. It was front-page news across the country and hailed as the most important archaeological discovery in Britain of the twentieth century. The only problem was that at that time, there was not the same sensitivity regarding our heritage as there is today and there seemed to be every prospect that once everybody who wished to had looked at them, then the ruins would simply be broken up and used as the foundation for the office buildings which were planned for the site. A hasty rescue plan was hatched, which entailed digging up what there was left of the temple and erecting it hundreds of yards away in an open-air position in front of another building. This was a far from ideal proposal, but it seemed to be either that or simply abandoning it to be broken up and concreted over.

The decision was made to move the remains of the temple and place them in Queen Victoria Street, about a hundred yards from where they had been found. This did not happen for eight years, and it was not until 1962 that the reconstruction was undertaken. Unfortunately, this was done without much input from archaeologists and the result was bizarre in the extreme. For example, the floor of the temple was replaced with very modern-looking crazy paving, of the kind one might have expected to see in a back garden at that time. Nor was that all. The reconstructed temple was set on a raised platform, so that any passing passenger on a bus could glance down upon it. The truth was, very few people even noticed the odd-looking ruin. The open position of the temple was horribly at odds with its original purpose. To understand why, we need to look a little at the origins of Mithraism.

A very ancient religion called Zoroastrianism originated in Persia, which is of course now more commonly known as Iran. The details need not concern us, but the essence of the religion is a titanic struggle between two gods; one good and the other evil. Mithras is a figure drawn from this mythology and adopted by well-to-do and powerful Romans. Somewhere between leaving Persia and arriving in Rome, Mithras acquired a mythological background of his own, which was unique to the Roman Empire. The central motif of this new faith was the tauroctony or slaying of a sacred bull by Mithras.

It must at once be said that we do not know all that much about the finer details of Mithraism as practised by the Romans. We know that the foundation myth entailed a bull being slain in a cave by Mithras and that various other symbolic images are usually present in the statues and reliefs which have been found. The one found in London in the nineteenth century, and which almost certainly came from the temple we shall be visiting, features a scorpion on the bull's genitals and a dog licking the blood from the wound which Mithras has inflicted on the animal's neck. What all this means is a complete mystery, but perhaps that is the way that it should be. Mithraism was, after all, a mystery region. It was not even known as Mithraism at the time which it was practised, but rather by allusive terms such as 'the Persian mysteries'.

That the temple in London stood on the banks of the Walbrook is no coincidence, for running water was necessary for worship. Once again, the reason for this is unknown. The easiest way to reach the Mithraeum in the street of Walbrook is to take the London Underground to Bank Station. On leaving the station, we walk down Walbrook, passing St Stephan's church on the left, before coming to the site of the temple on the right. It was when this new building was planned, as the European headquarters of the American media company Bloomberg, that it was decided to incorporate a space in the foundations to display the Mithraeum found here in 1954, almost exactly where it was originally. The result is little short of stunning. Mixed–media presentations take place throughout the day and details may be found in the appendix to this book.

To reach the Temple of Mithras, which is now on what was the Roman ground level, it is of course necessary to descend 20ft or so. The temple was built in the back garden of a wealthy citizen some time in the middle of the third century AD. The name of the man who caused it to be erected here is unknown, but we do know who paid for the altar, because of an inscription on the back of the tauroctony, which was found near here during the Victorian period and must surely have been displayed here. This was a man called Ulpius Silvanus. As we have already seen, paying for something of this kind might have been a bargain which this person had made with the deity, either in thanks for some piece of good fortune or as a gift because he was soliciting a favour from the gods.

Before going down the steps to visit the Mithraeum, it is worth sparing a few moments to examine the wall-high display case of Roman remains found when archaeologists from the Museum of London delved in the mud of the Walbrook, before the new building began to take shape. Among them is a very early written reference to London. As with the other early mentions of the city at which we have looked, it is interesting to note that this one too was found in a religious context.

When the temple was first found in the 1950s, Christianity was of far greater significance in Britain than is today the case and there was considerable excitement at the possibility that this might turn out to be one of the most ancient churches ever found anywhere in the world. It is understandable why at first glance it should have been taken for a church, because there are certainly points of similarity.

When we looked at the Romano-Celtic temple in Greenwich Park, we learned that in Roman religion generally, ordinary people were not permitted to enter the building where the god supposedly had his or her presence. They were limited to the enclosure around the temple and could perhaps hope to glimpse the god through the door of the temple. Only the priests themselves were allowed actually to go inside. This is very different from modern religious practice in Britain. These days, whether in churches, synagogues, mosques or Hindu temples, ordinary people expect to enter the building either for worship or prayer. Such an arrangement would have been seen as almost sacrilegious to the Romans, at least for the first few centuries of their time in this country. Mithraism, like Christianity, broke with this long-standing tradition.

When we enter a church, we are aware that although the area around the altar is especially sacred, that God is supposedly present in the entire building. This is, from what we are able to gather, how Roman worshippers of Mithras felt about their temple. It was this sort of thing which made Christians view Mithraism as a dangerous rival in the first few centuries after the death of Jesus. Most of the pagan cults were fairly irrational and easily refuted, but Mithraism presented a real challenge to Christians because of its almost uncanny similarity to their own faith. For one thing, the virtues which the followers of Mithras adhered to were very much the same as those observed by Christians. Men, for this was an exclusively male religion, had to follow strict principles in their private lives. They were enjoined to be honest, to abstain from sharp business practices and to eschew lies and deceit. The central part of their worship also involved a shared meal, which was very much like the communion of Christianity. Nor was that all.

Perhaps the most significant fixed date in the calendar for Christians is 25 December, when the birth of Jesus is celebrated. Mithras supposedly came forth from a rock, without having a mother, but this this event was also celebrated on 25 December. All this was a bit much for the Christians and they regarded Mithraism as being a devilish parody of their own religion and a far more dangerous religion that any of the other cults which were extant in Londinium.

The Mithraeum is today shrouded in darkness and the lights are always kept dimmed around the quiet hall in which it has been partially rebuilt. Illustration 53 shows the temple as it may be seen today. Looking at it now, it is little wonder that those who uncovered it in 1954 might have mistaken it for a church. There is the nave, lined with columns and with aisles on either side. There is a large container for water, whose purpose is unknown. This of course reminds us of the baptismal font which may be found in Anglican and Catholic churches, usually in a prominent position. Walking around the outside

53. The Temple of Mithras today.

of the temple, we find that at the back, behind where the altar would have been, is an apse. This is a semi-circular recess of the kind found in many churches. It may be seen in Illustration 54. In fact, in almost every way this building could have been the prototype for Christian churches, something else which would hardly be likely to endear the worshippers of Mithras to the average Christian.

The reason that the space in which the ruins of the temple have been rebuilt is kept gloomy and dark has something to do with both the style of worship in Mithraism and also the mythology which underlay it. It also explains why placing the reconstructed building on a raised plinth in the open air, as was done when it was repositioned in Queen Victoria Street in 1962, was spectacularly inappropriate. These temples were designed to be like caves and most of them were built partly underground. They were intended to be dark. This was partly to give them a mysterious and perhaps 'spooky' feel, but it was also a

54. The apse of the Temple of Mithras.

nod to the most basic myth of the religion, the slaying of the bull by Mithras, which took place in a cave. At the opposite end of the temple from the entrance was the most holy part of the building and it was here that the tauroctony would have been placed and illuminated with lamps. As with other such bas-reliefs of the time, traces of paint have been found on such sculptures, so we know that they were brightly coloured and as realistic as could be.

Nobody really knows what form services took in these temples, because a key part of the religion was mystery and secrecy. Perhaps the best modern parallel would be not with church services or anything of that kind, but rather meetings of Freemasons. There were rituals in the dark which were apparently designed to be scary and unnerving, but in what way, we do not know. Members were initiated into different grades, just as are Freemasons today. Ultimately, they were gatherings of well-to-do and important men, businessmen, army officers and so on, and they looked out for each other.

For some time, Christianity and Mithraism vied for mastery in Britain, with the result, as we know, that Christianity was triumphant. This was a very intolerant religion which could brook no rivals and so temples dedicated to other gods were attacked and either destroyed or converted into churches. This accounts of course for the way that various fragments of statues, images and paraphernalia relating to other faiths have been found buried or thrown down wells, to protect them from the irrational hatred of Christians.

One other temple complex should be mentioned, although there is today no trace of it; other than random blocks of carved stone in various museums. One of these may be seen in Illustration 59 (see page 210). It is an altar which depicts four mother goddesses and it was used in the building of the riverside wall near Blackfriars.

In 1974 and 1975, many blocks of stone were found during building work and archaeological excavations near Upper Thames Street, which marks the site of the water's edge of the Thames in Roman times. It was known that in the fourth century AD the authorities in Londinium had caused a wall to be built which protected the city from assault from the river. This was at a time that Saxon pirates and other irregular forces were becoming an increasing menace in the North Sea and were beginning to interfere with shipping as far south as the English Channel. There was a fear that ships might sail up the Thames and disgorge bands of heavily armed men who would then pillage and loot London. It was this anxiety of course which led to the construction of the bastions on the east side of the landward wall, which were intended to deter attack from forces landing in Essex and making their way overland to Londinium.

The archaeological excavations in Upper Thames Street eventually revealed a stretch of wall along what was once the riverbank which stretched for over 300ft. Some of the wall had rested on foundations of wooden stakes which had been driven into the mud. This indicated that its construction was more hurried than that of the better-known wall at which we have looked, which encircled the city to the east, west and north. Those building the riverside wall wanted to have the thing up and in place as quickly as could be managed, probably in a matter of weeks. Dendrochronological analysis showed that the wooden foundation was made from trees which were cut down in 330 AD. The stonework of the wall revealed an interesting story, because most of the fifty-two blocks which were recovered proved to come from two constructions which had been dismantled and looted in order to build the wall.

It will be remembered that the bastions which were added to the wall on the east side were filled with the remains of tombstones, statues and mausolea. The less distance which one has to haul heavy blocks of stone, the better, and when the riverside wall was being erected near what is now the vicinity of Blackfriars, there lay close at hand a most convenient source of building materials. After piecing together the various bits of stone, archaeologists found that the great majority of them came from two structures. One of these was a large decorative arch and the other was a screen showing various gods and goddesses. The arch also depicted pagan deities, including Minerva and Jupiter. It was deduced that both arch and the screen most probably stood close at hand to where the riverside wall was built and that they were part of a temple complex which stood in and around the area now occupied by Blackfriars railway station.

It has been hypothesized that the monumental arch acted as a gateway to what might be thought of as a temple 'district', where a group of temples would provide for the religious needs of almost any worshippers. The altar with the images of the four mothers would have been held sacred by both Romans and Celts, so clearly the area catered not just for those who revered the traditional Roman pantheon. An inscription mentioned the restoration of a temple to the Egyptian goddess Isis as well. Other references to this temple have been found and it seems likely that it stood in the precinct near Blackfriars.

The temples which were broken up to build the riverside wall were probably grouped together for convenience. We have already seen that there was, until the coming of Christianity, no friction between the different religions which were practised in Londinium and people often worshipped more than one set of gods. Even an Egyptian goddess fitted in smoothly to this laid-back approach to worship. It was considered quite the thing to sacrifice to more than one god, just to be sure of honouring the one who actually helped in your life. The fragments which were recovered from the fallen wall which lined the riverbank in that part of London suggest strongly that at least three places of worship stood near this spot, catering for all comers.

It is a pity that no trace remains today to indicate just where these temples actually stood. The supposed religious district could have been established anywhere between the top of Ludgate Hill, where St Paul's Cathedral now stands, and the river. Mention of the cathedral leads us naturally to the subject of the next chapter, which is an investigation of the rumour that a huge Roman cathedral was built in Londinium, one which was almost as long as St Paul's itself and which was quite lost to sight until a quarter of a century ago.

Chapter 12

The Mystery of London's Roman 'Cathedral'

No book on the subject of Roman London could be complete without a discussion of the supposed large church or cathedral which was, according to some reports, discovered during the early 1990s. Although many people have heard of this, information is remarkably difficult to come by and even the location of what was claimed at the time to be one of the greatest archaeological discoveries ever made in the city is not easy to pin down. However, I shall be describing the site in detail in this chapter and giving directions for those readers who feel that they would like at least to know where the place is.

In 1995, a remarkable news story broke in Britain. On Monday, 3 April, the *Independent* newspaper published a long article beneath the headline, 'Archaeologists unearth capital's first cathedral'. There followed an account of a 300ft-long building dating from the second half of the fourth century which had been unearthed in central London. It was an extraordinary story and the first few paragraphs seem to indicate that this was no vague and insubstantial theory, but solid and verifiable fact;

> Archaeologists have discovered what appears to have been London's first cathedral. Research on Tower Hill suggests that in the 4th-century AD, the Romans built a massive church overlooking the city.
>
> The building would have been one of the world's largest early churches. Only those of Italy and Trier in Germany were bigger.

Months of analysis of data from excavations on the site have revealed the existence of a 100m-long, 50m-wide building almost identical in design though slightly larger than the church of St Thecla in Milan, the largest church in the then capital of the Roman Empire.

This was, to say the very least, intriguing. The Temple of Mithras had caused a stir when it was discovered and crowds of people flocked to see it, partly because it was thought that it might actually have been an early church. This building though was in a different league. The temple found in 1954 had been only 60ft long, barely a fifth of the size of this huge structure, which was as long as the front of Buckingham Palace.

A description was also given of how lavish and ostentatious this late Roman building had been. Readers were told that it had been built from previously used masonry and that this had been covered with black marble. The interior was apparently plastered and then painted with designs in red, white, grey, pink and yellow. All in all, it sounded a most dramatic and exciting find. Nor was it a maverick archaeologist who was telling the newspapers all about this. Far from being some latter-day Indiana Jones, David Sankey had for the past seven years been the senior archaeologist at the Museum of London.

There was considerable interest in this story and people waited to hear more about the business, perhaps being told where this discovery had been made and when they would be able to visit the 'cathedral'. Surely, this was at least on a par with the Temple of Mithras and there had been no shortage of people at that time who wished to view the remains. But nothing more was heard about the matter. Indeed, googling the subject today will usually bring up only that one single story from the *Independent*, and nothing else.

This silence following what sounded like a major announcement was curious and did not go unnoticed, even in Parliament. Three and a half months after the news broke, an MP rose in the House of Commons to ask a question of the Secretary of State for National Heritage. On 18 July, Martin Redmond said that he wished to ask the Secretary of State, 'What assistance her Department is giving to the Museum of London archaeology service's excavations on Tower Hill of the late Roman church; and if she will make a statement?' The reply was short and wholly uninformative:

> My department does, of course, give funds to the Museum of London but no extra assistance is being provided by my department for these excavations. I am pleased to learn that provision has been made for archaeological excavation and analysis of the site, and that this has led to the discovery of Roman and later remains.

And that, as far as the general public was concerned, was that. No mention was ever made again in the newspapers of this wonderful discovery and there was no follow-up at all to the tantalizing revelations which had been made. Those who believe in conspiracy theories might well think that something was being hushed up, so complete was the silence after that initial news story and mention in Parliament.

Almost 30 years have now passed since first we heard of the cathedral and yet most of us know no more now than we did then. What happened to the remains of the huge building? Was it really a cathedral? Was the story deliberately suppressed? Almost nothing can be found today about this, even on the internet, beyond those two sources.

Before going any further, perhaps it would be interesting to know just where this discovery was made, since information about that too is all but impossible to track down after so many years have passed. The excavation took place while the foundations for a building were being prepared. This building is called Novotel and it is an hotel which opened in 2000. To find it, one leaves Tower Hill Tube station and immediately in front is an open space, called Trinity Square Gardens. To the right of this is Trinity House and behind that is Novotel. It is bounded by Pepys Street, Savage Gardens and Coopers Row. This then is where David Sankey found the building about which we have been reading.

Fully to appreciate what it would mean if a Roman church of such a great size had really been identified in the centre of London, we need to think a little about Christianity in Roman Britain and also about the nature of architecture at that time and how it affected our ideas today about the appearance of ecclesiastical buildings.

We do not know when Christianity first reached Britain. The martyrdom of St Alban is generally thought to have taken place about the middle of the third century, so by 250 AD or thereabouts there were not only Christians in this the country, but enough to make it worthwhile persecuting them, to stop the spread of the religion. The first solid evidence, as opposed to vague legends, is provided by some plates and spoons, evidently used in church services, which came to light during the ploughing of a field near the English town of Peterborough in 1974. These were marked with the symbol known as the Chi Rho, these being the first two letter of the Greek word Christos or Christ. Superimposed on each other, they were used as a code by early Christians. Illustration 55 shows a mosaic which features a cleanly shaven Jesus, with the Chi Rho visible behind his head, forming a kind of halo. This was found in a Roman villa in Dorsetshire and dates from the fourth century.

No signs of Christianity though have ever come to light in London dating from the time of the Roman occupation. In 2016, it was claimed that a shard of Roman pottery found in the London suburb of Brentford has a Chi Rho scratched on the base, but this has been disputed. Some experts say that it is more likely to be a solar sign, a graffito common in various parts of the world.

The evidence of Christianity in London at that time which has come to light is of two kinds. The first is archaeological, but this is doubtful and open to other interpretations. For instance, we looked at the pagan cult items retrieved from the well beneath Southwark

55. An early image of Jesus from Roman Britain.

Cathedral and saw that one possibility is that they had been damaged by Christians and that the devotees of whatever faith revered them had cast them into the well to prevent them being wholly destroyed. The same explanation has been advanced for the fact that the images of various deities from the Temple of Mithras in London seem to have been buried in the same way, perhaps to protect them from Christians.

Christianity was like no religion which had previously been seen in Britain. Other faiths were tolerant and had no desire to attack anybody following a different god or goddess. Some people belonged to more than one religion and nobody found this at all strange. This is why the

Romans did not fall out with the Celts about their religious practices. Roman temples might be dedicated to various gods and even those who practiced Mithraism were not debarred from honouring other deities beside Mithras. Christians though, had quite another perspective on this. Their Bible teaches them that their god is jealous and becomes enraged at the sight of people serving any other god but him. The very first of the Ten Commandments, the cornerstone of both the Jewish and Christian faiths, is, 'You shall have no other gods before Me'. The second is, 'You shall not make for yourself a carved image'. So it was that pagan temples fell foul of Christianity on two counts, since not only were the dedicated to other gods, they contained images of these supposed divinities. It is for this reason that broken and burnt statues of gods are taken to be evidence of Christian intolerance. More than that, if they can in some way be dated, then the rise of the influence of Christianity in the country can be charted. This is one kind of clue about when Christianity became a force to be reckoned with in Roman Britain. There is another.

In 314 AD, the year after Christianity was made a legal religion in the Roman Empire, meaning its adherents no longer had to meet in secret, a council of churches met in the city of Arles, in what is now France. They intended to thrash out various matters about which there was controversy. For instance, at that time the date of Easter was decided by local churches, but it was ruled at the Council of Arles, that everybody should celebrate Easter on the same day, throughout the entire world. Records show that three British bishops attended the council, from London, York and Lincoln. That there should be a bishop in London at that time makes it a reasonable guess that there was a church of some kind there, where he would be able to hold services.

The reports which emerged in 1995 about the enormous building which had been found claimed that part of the evidence that it was a church or cathedral was that it was identical in plan to a Roman church which we know of in Milan, called the Church of St Thecla.

This is a Roman church which was built in the fourth century AD. It was a rectangular building with an apse, but then so too were many buildings at that time, whether sacred or profane, for ecclesiastical use or day-to-day business. The Temple of Mithras was rectangular with an apse and so too was Londinium's basilica. This sounds like a fairly vague resemblance at best.

There is another difficulty when identifying a building from the fourth century positively as being a church, and this touches upon where our ideas of what 'looks' like a church come from in the first place. If we are not careful, then looking at a Roman building and deciding that it has the external appearance of a church can lead us astray. This is what nearly happened of course when the Temple of Mithras was first revealed in 1954. It was a rectangular building with an apse at one end and columns which suggested to people the nave of a church. Perhaps we need to ask ourselves why some buildings suggest to us that they might be churches, rather than farmhouses or barns.

In 1989, the remains of a Roman building were excavated in the Hampshire village of Meonstock. It was at first very difficult to know what this building had been. What was certain was that it had been constructed in the early fourth century and had collapsed some time after 353 AD, a coin of this date being found beneath the fallen ruins. The reconstructed façade of the building showed that it would have been roughly 50ft high and perhaps 40ft wide. The appearance of what was thought to be an agricultural storehouse on an estate associated with a nearby villa was quite extraordinary. To begin with, it was colourful, being composed of white plaster and grey flints, with tiles set in patterns to give a red-and-white striped effect. Then too, there were three windows with round arches, these windows being divided by classical pillars in the Ionic style, topped with greenstone capitals. Above these windows was a blind arcade, part of which is shown in Illustration 56. This is now preserved in the British Museum. The overall effect was that of a Romanesque church of the eleventh

56. Part of a barn in Roman Britain.

century. Not only did the façade of the building appear identical to certain known churches of that period, but the interior space itself had been divided into aisles, just like a church.

If this building had been found in a city, rather than near an isolated villa in the middle of the countryside, it is by no means impossible that it might have been interpreted as some kind of church. Its location, though, on a farming estate, made this very unlikely. It was in fact a barn; simply somewhere to store grain and hay, and perhaps to shelter animals in. It had just been made to look as visually appealing as possible, whether by some whim of the landowner or as part of a tradition in domestic architecture. This gave rise to a theory, which has yet to be confirmed, that the style and appearance of ecclesiastical buildings in Europe might have been inspired by or modelled upon Roman vernacular architecture. In other words, those building the earliest churches in Europe might simply have looked at granaries and barns and decided that such buildings would be eminently suitable, both in design and appearance, for gathering large groups of people together for worshipping God.

It will of course be remembered from the last chapter that the procedure in Romano-Celtic temples was different from Christian worship. For the pagans, the body of people did not actually enter the building itself, the *cella*, but stood outside in the sacred enclosure. It was obvious that if Christians gathered together indoors to practice their religion, then something larger than a *cella* would be needed. Perhaps these pioneers simply looked at a few barns and thought that such a place would do perfectly for what they had in mind.

This brings us back to the Roman 'cathedral' which might once have stood on Tower Hill. With all the excitement about the earliest place of Christian worship in London possibly being revealed, few people were at all keen to hear the more balanced view of the case which emerged a year or two later, when the idea was mooted that rather than a church, this had in fact been no more than a granary or barn. So it was that in June 1995, the respected magazine *British Archaeology* reported as fact the existence of a Roman church in London, saying,

A MASSIVE late Roman church, possibly London's first cathedral, has been found by archaeologists on Tower Hill. The 4th-century church is almost identical in design to the church of St Thecla in Milan – the biggest church in what was then the capital of the Roman Empire – but the London church is larger. The building, excavated by David Sankey of the Museum of London Archaeology Service, seems to have been built between AD350 and AD400 out of masonry reused from other buildings. It was decorated in part by a veneer of black marble, its walls were painted red, white, grey, pink and yellow, and its floor was made of broken tiles in cement. The church may have been built by Magnus Maximus, who used

Britain as a power base to become western emperor between AD383 and AD388. It was burned down in the 5th century.

Sixteen years later though, when the excitement, one might almost say hysteria, had died down a little, the *Transactions of the London and Middlesex Archaeological Society* contained a paper by Dr James Gerrard, Senior Lecturer in Roman Archaeology at Newcastle University, the title of which was, CATHEDRAL OR GRANARY? THE ROMAN COINS FROM COLCHESTER HOUSE, CITY OF LONDON. This was the first hint that anybody in the outside world had that there might not after all have been a cathedral in London during the fourth century.

The gist of Gerrard's piece was that the large building which was investigated could just as well have been a barn as it was a church. At that time, a tax was levied on grain and this was paid in grain, which was brought to Londinium and stored for a while there. This could conceivably have been done in this structure, which certainly resembled a barn as much as it did a church, perhaps for reasons which we looked at above. There were two things though which might indicate a religious rather than secular use for the site. One was the number of coins found there. Large numbers of coins are typically found at the sites of Roman-Celtic temples and these depositions form a particular pattern over the centuries, with numbers fluctuating from one period to another. It seems that the coins at this site might accord with the pattern seen at other ritual and religious sites in Roman Britain. The other curious thing was a type of pottery found buried beneath the granary or church.

At various ritual and religious sites dating from the Roman occupation of Britain, a distinctive type of bowl has been found, which archaeologists have, with a singular lack of imagination, termed CAM306. In London, these vessels have been found at both the Walbrook Mithraeum and also the temple site in Tabard Square in Southwark. They have been unearthed too in Colchester at the site of both a Mithraeum and also what has been taken to be a Christian church. It has been said that the presence of CAM306 bowls should be regarded as important as cult statues in deciding whether or not some site had a religious significance for the Romans.

What then can we say in the end about the famous 'cathedral'? Perhaps the strangest aspect of the business is the way that the idea flamed brightly for a few months almost 30 years ago, before fading and dying away. There was so much excitement about the supposed Roman church, but then everybody seemed to lose interest. The evidence today is no less strong than it was in 1995, but it seems that the enthusiasm for the notion of old cathedrals is less than it was then. The most we can say is that it is altogether possible that there was once a Roman church in the streets near Trinity Gardens, but then again, it is almost as likely that there was only some kind of grand barn. Perhaps in the future, further excavations in the area will bring forth further, and it is to be hope more definite, evidence which might decide the matter one way or another.

Chapter 13

The Roman Way of Death

Despite the fact that there were at least five Roman cemeteries in what is now central London, the actual places which one can visit in the capital with evidence on the ground of Roman funerals and burial practices is exceedingly sparse. Having said this, there is one site within the boundary of Greater London which is quite extraordinarily well-preserved and this makes up in some measure for the paucity of remains to be seen elsewhere.

Before exploring those parts of London where the Roman dead lie buried, we must recapitulate some of what was said in previous chapters. The Romans had, in common with some other ancient cultures, a taboo on disposing of their dead in the same area where they themselves lived. This may have been for reasons of hygiene or it might equally well have been because there was some superstitious dread of sharing a common space with the dead, for fear of ghosts or other supernatural reasons. For whatever reason, it led to the custom of establishing burial grounds outside cities. In the case of walled cities, as London became, it was found convenient for cemeteries to be located right outside the gates leading into the city. There were two reasons for this. One was that when one is conducting a funeral, then the less distance that it is necessary to travel from one's home to the place of interment the better. There is also of course the consideration that anybody entering or leaving the city will be obliged to pass memorials to the dead and that if you could manage it, the mausolea of your own dead relatives and friends might be so prominently placed that their names would jump out at travellers. This was a form of immortality, a way of ensuring that the dead person was not forgotten.

It led to the development of something like cities of the dead, through which one had to travel in order to reach the place of the living. The best example of this strange arrangement was not in this country, but on the road between Rome and Brindisi, known as the Appian Way.

Illustration 57 is of the outskirts of Rome when the empire was at its height. At first sight, it might appear to show a city street, with tall buildings lining either side of the road. Look closer though and you will see that these are not buildings for the living, but rather mausolea and tombs. It is in fact a necropolis, a city of the dead. Entering Rome by that route meant walking or riding past sepulchres which were grander than the homes of many poor people in Rome itself. Apart from making sure that the memory of the dead did not fade, this odd practice was also motivated by a strange belief current at that time that the dead in some way enjoyed the company of those passing to and fro. They actually liked hearing the living as they passed by, talking perhaps, and this enabled them, vicariously of course, to maintain a link with the real world. Of course, the tombs on the approaches to

57. Rome's Appian Way.

Londinium were not on such a magnificent scale as this, but they were still very noticeable and it would have been impossible to enter the city without seeing and being aware of them.

From the earliest days of their civilization the Romans believed in survival after death, which has been of great benefit to archaeologists and has aided enormously in our understanding of Roman life. This is because graves often included things which might be of use to the dead person in the afterlife. So it was that food and drink, household goods and favourite possessions would be carefully buried with the corpse or incinerated ashes of the dead person. Many of the artifacts which we see in our museums from Roman London were found in graves. It is probably fair to say that a good deal of what we know about the way of *life* in Roman London has come from examining the way of *death*. So it is that have recovered complete tea sets, or the Roman equivalent, from graves, together with make-up and textiles. Dice and gaming pieces, which were thoughtfully interred with their owner to while away their long evenings in the afterlife, have also been found. This is the case even when the corpses were burned to ashes and packed into a vase or urn for burial.

In the early years of Londinium the Roman dead were more likely to be cremated and the ashes buried than they were to be interred as intact corpses. However, fashions change in funerals and beliefs in the nature of the afterlife as in every other field of human affairs, and by the end of the Roman occupation of Britain, it was the custom to place the corpse in a sarcophagus or coffin and then bury that in the ground. A number of such sarcophagi have been dug up in London.

One grave which we are able to visit is that of a teenage girl who died in the later years of Roman London and was buried just inside the city gate at Bishopsgate. Finding this grave and seeing the memorial to her death could hardly be simpler, for she is buried beneath one of the most notable buildings in the City of London. This is 30 St Mary Axe, more commonly known as 'the Gherkin' due to its unusual shape; it is visually similar to such a small, pickled cucumber. What is remarkable about this burial is that it took place not outside the city wall, as was customary, but rather well within it. Nobody knows the reason for this unusual proceeding.

On 10 April 1992, the IRA detonated the largest bomb to explode in London since the Blitz in 1940. It consisted of over a ton of explosives, packed into a van which was parked outside the Baltic Exchange in the heart of the financial district of the City of London. Three people were killed in the explosion and the physical damage caused to buildings in the area was immense. The Baltic Exchange itself, a well-known landmark which had been completed in 1903, was destroyed. Plans to rebuild it came to nothing and it was agreed that a new and distinctive building would be erected on the site. This was to be the famous 'Gherkin'. When the site was being cleared and foundations dug in 1995, a Roman grave was found. Archaeologists for the Museum of London were surprised, because this area was well within the city wall of Roman London.

The body found within the grave was that of a girl aged between 13 and 17. She had been laid on her back and her arms crossed over her chest. From the style of burial, that is to say the disposition of the body, and one or two other clues, it was determined that this burial had taken place between 350 to 400 AD. After being taken to the Museum of London for some years, it was decided, upon completion of the new building, that it would be more fitting and decent to reinter the girl where she had been found; that is to say at the base of the so-called 'Gherkin'. So it was that in April 2007, 12 years after she had been dug up, the girl was returned to her original resting place. A service was held at the church of St Botolph Aldgate, following which a procession carried the remains to the Gherkin and they were laid to rest once more.

To visit the grave of the Roman girl, it is necessary to take a train to Liverpool Street Station and then to leave the station at the exit to Bishopsgate. Liverpool Street Station is built upon the site of part of the Roman cemetery which lay by the road here. Bishopsgate, the street in which we are now standing, was part of Ermine Street, the Roman Road leading north from Londinium. We turn right on leaving the station and begin walking south, towards the 'Gherkin'. We are now heading towards on the gates in the Roman city wall. On our right, we pass the church of St Botolph-without-Bishopsgate. In this context 'without' means 'outside'. This means that the church was outside the gate in the wall, which was still here long after the departure of the Romans. We come to the point where the gate once stood when we reach the main road which cuts across Bishopsgate here. It will no doubt be remembered from our walk along the line of the Roman wall that it ran along the line of the street both left and right.

We cross the road and turn left, down Camomile Street and begin walking along it. The wall would have been on our left and one of the bastions was built into the wall here towards the end of Londinium's existence when it was menaced by the Saxons. Illustration 35 (see page 98) shows the foundation of one such bastion which we visited; it was near the Tower of London. These bastions, which mounted heavy ballistas, were built hurriedly to combat an emergency and so utilized whatever material lay readily at hand. For those preparing the bastion here, there was a very obvious source of stone which was simply waiting to be collected. This was the cemetery which lay only a short distance away on either side of the streets which we have just followed from Liverpool Street Station. One instance of this use of monuments and tombs may be seen in the statue of the Roman soldier, seen in Illustration 29 (see page 82). This was found in the remains of the bastion here in Camomile Street and had clearly been looted from a memorial.

The second turning on the right is called Bury Street and we cross the road and walk along it. It will lead us to the 'Gherkin' on the right-hand side, looming above us like a spaceship from a science-fiction film. The base of this building is surrounded by long, low blocks of slate-grey stone and on one of these, the following words are engraved;

To the spirits of the dead	DIS MANIBVS
the Unknown young girl	PUELLA ICOGNITA
from Roman London	LONDININESIS
lies buried here	HIC SEPVLTA EST

Nearby, another inscription records the names of the three victims of the IRA bombing. One of these was also a teenage girl, 15-year-old Danielle Carter.

Although the burial within the walls violated the strict letter of Roman religious law, there is some reason to suppose that in later years the rules were disregarded. The population of Londinium was falling sharply towards the end of its existence and perhaps this kind of thing was more widespread at that time. It is certainly the case that urns and vases of human ashes have been found within the city walls.

While we are in this part of London, it might be worth walking a short distance to the site of one of the cemeteries about which we have been thinking. If we walk back to Bishopsgate, then we are once again at the northern gate to the Roman city, the one from which Ermine Street began. Walking back towards Liverpool Street Station, although remaining on this side of the road, we are now leaving Londinium and making our way along the road to Lincoln and York, both of which were Roman cities. Once past the station we take a turning on the right called Artillery Lane. If we walk along the entire length of this narrow street, we shall find a turning on our left which is called Crispin Street. Before walking along Crispin Street, it is worth pausing for a moment and looking at the shopfront of 56–58 Artillery Lane. This is the oldest shopfront in the whole of London. The building itself is seventeenth-century, and it was converted into a shop some 300 years ago.

The modern development which is on our left-hand side as we walk up Crispin Street was built around the turn of the present century. It covers a large area and before building started, archaeologists were afforded an unprecedented opportunity to examine in detail a good expanse of central London and see what had happened there over the last few thousand years. Similar excavations have also taken place north of here, around the other side of the old Spitalfields Market, and many hidden aspects of life in London were revealed. If we walk along Crispin Street until we come to the market ahead of us and then turn left, we shall be able to see something very interesting. Once we pass the market hall, there is a plaza to the right called Bishop's Square and large-scale archaeological research here also brought to light many Roman burials. This land was all part of the cemetery which stretched along Ermine Street. Before we look at what was found here from that time, there is something curious in Bishop's Square which is also connected with burial and the dead, although at a somewhat later date than the Romans.

If we walk along this open space, we come to a glass-covered area which provides a view to below ground level. It is of an old building, the oldest in this part of London. Steps allow one to descend and examine it more closely. This was a charnel house and it dates back to the thirteenth century. A charnel house was somewhere to store human bones for which there was no longer any room in a burial ground. If a skeleton was found while digging a new grave, then it would be taken to the charnel house and so stored with dignity.

Hundreds of Roman graves were found in this area, but perhaps the one which is most remembered is that of the young woman whose remains were found in the first unopened Roman sarcophagus to be found in London for a hundred years. It was immediately obvious to those who found this great stone chest that somebody very special had been interred here and so indeed it proved. Within the stone box lay a beautifully-made lead coffin, decorated with relief sculptures of scallop shells. This may be seen in Illustration 58 and it is currently on display at the Museum of London. It was what was found within that coffin which excited the imagination not only of archaeologists and historians, but also ordinary Londoners. The discovery of the contents of the sarcophagus in 1999 seemed to stir that same kind of

58. The coffin of the 'Spitalfields' Princess'.

fascination which the finding of the Temple of Mithras had, 45 years earlier. When first the coffin and the remains of the young woman within it were put on display to the public at the Museum of London, the size of the queues to see were almost unbelievable. It is estimated that 10,000 people flocked there in the first few days, simply to file past the open coffin to view the skeleton. For somebody whose name is unknown to us, it was an extraordinary event.

Few bodies from the Roman period which have been found in this country were subjected to as much rigorous investigation as was that of the woman dubbed by some the 'Spitalfields Princess'. The reason for such a nickname is not hard to guess. The young women, in her early twenties, was delicate; one person who examined her skeleton compared her to a ballet dancer. It was what remained of her clothes though which really gave a clue about her background and made it obvious that she came from a wealthy, and very probably aristocratic, family. When she died, around 350 AD, her body was dressed before burial in a silk tunic. The material for this would have had to be imported all the way from China and would accordingly have been fantastically expensive. Nor was that all. Woven through the fabric were threads of gold and there were even traces of Tyrian purple in the coffin, a very costly dye which might have come from a blanket.

Being buried in such rich and extravagant clothes certainly seems to suggest that the young woman, if not actually a princess, certainly came from a very well-to-do background. It is possible that she was so beautifully attired for her own funeral because she might have been displayed to mourners in an open coffin as part of the funeral ceremony. Although this practice has almost vanished in modern Britain, some ethnic groups in the country still favour open coffins, which are displayed in a church or at home before and during the funeral. Caribbeans sometimes engage in this practice and so do Irish people, and great care is taken in selecting the dead person's favourite clothes and jewellery and making sure that the hair and make-up, in the case of a woman, are as she would have wanted them to be.

Bay leaves were also found in the coffin; incredibly, they were still intact and recognizable after the better part of 2,000 years. There were expensive personal items too, delicate glass phials which probably once contained perfume or oils. There was also a cosmetic kit made of jet. Other organic material consisted of pine and pistachio oil. It is thought that this might have been poured around the coffin like air freshener, thus reinforcing the idea that this would have been an open-coffin funeral. Without embalming, decomposition can set in swiftly with a corpse and with that process comes an awful smell.

The remains of the Spitalfields woman were also examined by testing the enamel in her teeth for isotopes which would enable scientists to say where she had grown up. DNA was also extracted from the bones and tested. The conclusions all tended to the same end, that this was an important woman from a wealthy family. She had almost certainly grown up in Rome itself and come to Britain as an adult. Her teeth showed that in childhood, she had suffered from a serious illness which temporarily halted her growth.

Armed with this information, it was perhaps inevitable that a few guesses should be made about the identity of this high-status young woman. One possibility is that she was the wife of a governor of part of Britain or perhaps of one of those in charge of later Roman Britain, a so-called *vicarius Britanniarum*. The truth is of course that we shall probably never know for certain.

In Chapter 3, we visited the site of another Roman burial, one which some people feel has great significance. This was beneath St Bride's Church in Fleet Street. There was of course a vast Roman cemetery outside the city gate and it has been estimated that thousands of burials took place here. The church was severely damaged during the Blitz in 1940; it was restored after the end of the Second World War. Apart from finding that it had been built on the site of an earlier Roman building, those examining the ground beneath the crypt found the burial of a woman which dated from the later centuries of the Roman occupation. Her grave had had a tile placed on it, a practice which has been noted at other Roman burials in East Anglia. From this and various other indications, for instance that she had been laid in an east-west position, it was concluded by those connected with the church that this was a Christian burial, which would make it the earliest such ever identified in this country.

It has to be said that despite St Bride's making this claim on their website and advertising it in guided tours of the church and crypt, there seems to be some doubt about the matter. Most old churches are keen to prove that they are the most ancient in the area or city and St Bride's is no exception. There is stiff competition in London for the title of the oldest church and St Bride's feels perhaps that this supposed Christian burial gives them a distinct edge. Some stonework in the crypt is labelled as dating from the sixth century, although there is some dispute about this, perhaps with the same end in mind, that is to say staking a claim. Of course, there is no question but that when St Bride's was originally founded here, the entire area would have been full of graves, as far as the eye could see. Among the later burials, it is entirely possible that there were Christians. The best verdict we can render in this question is probably the old Scots one of 'Not proven'.

While we are talking of St Bride's, it is worth mentioning that it may just be possible to see some of the Romans who were buried near the church, due to a curious circumstance. In Spitalfields, we saw what was left of a charnel house which has once stood there. In the crypt at St Bride's, there are not one but two charnel houses. Both were opened up when the place was being rebuilt after the Blitz. One contained the remains of people who had died during the Great Plague in the late seventeenth century and also victims of the cholera outbreak in nineteenth-century London. Most of these skeletons were in coffins with nameplates and so could readily be identified. There was, however, a second charnel house dating back to the medieval period. This contained many thousands of human bones and skulls, stacked neatly in heaps. This place has not been fully excavated, because the piles of bones stretch deep into the ground beneath the crypt. These are bones which were dug up many hundreds of years ago when graves were being dug in the churchyard and were then carried here to be piled up and cared for with reverence. Considering the number of Roman burials which took place in and around this area, it would be very surprising if some of these bones were not the remains of Romans. It is unlikely though that this charnel house will ever be properly examined, because there are simply too many bones here. Readers who wish to see the charnel house for themselves will be obliged to book a tour with the church, as it is impossible simply to walk in and view them.

It is time to see what those monuments which lined the roads leading into Londinium would have looked like before they were dismantled for building materials. By great good fortune, three such tombs still remain in the Greater London area. The bad news is that they are in a private garden and may only be viewed by the general public once or twice a year. In Illustration 3 (see page ix), we are able to see what they look like today and it really is quite strange to see part of what was once a street of tombs, of the kind which we might expect to encounter in Pompeii, set in the countryside on the outskirts of London.

The tombs at which we shall now look were built near a villa rather than a city, but they are identical in design to those found elsewhere across the Roman world and there is no reason to suppose them to be any different from those which would have been found outside the gates of Londinium. To reach them, it will be necessary either to drive to Hayes or to take a train from Lewisham in south London to there.

The chief reason that people have tombs built is so that their relatives or friends will not be forgotten. This is as true today as it was during the Roman occupation of Britain. A large and elaborate mausoleum tells those who pass by it two important things. In the first place, it tells them that whoever is contained within the structure must have come from an important family who cared enough about him to go to all the trouble of building something like this. It is, in short, a classic example of what would, in the twentieth century, come to be known as 'conspicuous consumption'. The second important function that such structures serve is to perpetuate the name of a family. This certainly benefits the living, raising their profile, as we would say today, but also furnishing the dead with a little immortality in this life, as well as the next. As long as the name is not forgotten, they can be said to live on, in a sense. This is why we refer to people like Shakespeare as 'immortal', of course. Having thought a little about the purpose of the tombs, it is time to see those at Keston, which although technically in London, lie on the very edge of Kent.

The three mausolea at Keston date from the third century AD and were first discovered in the nineteenth century. Nothing much was done about them at that time though. A stone coffin was found in the vicinity at about the same time and this too is on display, near the tombs. Although no Roman city or even settlement is nearby, the remains of a large villa, which evidently belonged to a prosperous family, has been unearthed. This has not been properly excavated though and has since been covered in earth again, to protect it from the elements, in the hope that at some future date it will be possible to investigate fully. It is assumed that the tombs are connected in some way with the villa. The tombs may be seen in Illustration 3 (see page ix) and there really is nothing like them anywhere else in the country. As we have seen, the monuments and gravestones on the edge of Roman London were plundered at will and it is reasonable to guess that a similar fate befell those on the fringes of other cities. Those at Keston are only low, stubby structures today, but they give us an idea of the size and solidity of such things. These were built to last, as indeed they have done for the better part of 2,000 years.

The Keston remains were systematically excavated during digs beginning in 1967. As a result, we are able to form a good idea about what they would have looked like when they were first built. The tombs outside the city gates of Londinium were probably similar in appearance. When finished, and before they were, like so many other bits of Roman brickwork and masonry, looted for material to use in other building projects, they would have stood perhaps 15 or 20ft in height. We return to a subject upon which we have already touched and that is the subconscious image we have of ancient Roman cities as having many dazzling white things, like buildings and statues. Obviously, the Romans were really just as fond of colourful surroundings as we are today and this can be seen when we consider what fragments of plaster unearthed around the tombs at Keston reveal. This is that they were originally painted bright red. It is an intriguing vision; the green, pastoral landscape, with 20ft-high red pillars rising from it. It would certainly be a good way of attracting the attention of passing travellers to the memorials of those who lay interred there.

Perhaps this gives us some notion of what the cemeteries close to Londinium might have looked like. Picture a road passing through a forest of 20ft columns painted red and various statues in which the dead person was shown in vivid and realistic colours. This might well clash with our ingrained ideas about Roman times, but it does tie in more with what the evidence actually suggests.

In the chapter on the Roman wall which once encircled London, we visited every gate and so automatically passed the sites of the chief burial grounds. It was impossible to enter Londinium overland without being compelled to travel through one of those cemeteries. Picture the scene as we approach the city. We have been travelling past green fields and through forests. When we are within sight of the city wall, splashes of bright colours, mainly red, catch our attention. Long before we reach the city gate, we come to the first tombs. They tower above us, some of them at least 20ft high. They are garish and designed with one purpose only in mind, which is to attract our attention. The tallest ones are all clustered along both sides of the road and it is a somewhat uncanny experience to make our way between these brightly painted structures, some of them reaching to the height of the gutters on a modern semi-detached house. It is like walking through a city of the dead. It is impossible not to notice some of the statues, nor to resist the temptation to stop and read some of the inscriptions, which are on white marble slabs and the incised letters carefully picked out in red paint.

These monuments then would surely have succeeded in their primary aim, which was to attract the attention of the living and make sure that the names of the dead were not allowed to be forgotten. Of course, the cemeteries north of the river were not the only ones, nor even the most interesting. South of Southwark, there were both temples and a large cemetery. The tombs which lay either side of

Watling Street as it approached Londinium, we know quite a bit about. There is not much to see these days if we walk along Borough High Street and the Great Dover Road, which is where part of this burial ground was to be found, but there is some reason to suppose that the land around here had been used in this way, for temples and tombs, even before the Romans arrived. By great good fortune, we can investigate some tombs which are still visible today and also lie near the route of Watling Street.

We are most of us aware that Salisbury Plain was what is known as ritual landscape, that is to say that it is a tract of land which is scattered with monuments and burial mounds which make the whole place special and spiritual in some way. It may surprise readers to learn that such a landscape exists in London and may be visited by travelling on the Docklands Light Railway. It predates the Roman invasion, but was adopted by the newcomers and accorded almost as much reverence as the native Celts gave it. Even more interestingly, its special status lingered on after the end of Roman London and it was also thought to be a holy place by the pagan Saxons. We shall consider only the aspect of this site as it touches upon the burial of the dead, although the site of a Romano-Celtic temple lies nearby and is almost certainly part of the same landscape.

Taking the Docklands Light Railway, get off at the station for the *Cutty Sark*, called, unsurprisingly, Cutty Sark (for Maritime Greenwich). Turn left when you leave the station and then walk along until you reach the road, after passing Waterstones bookshop on your left-hand side. Cross the road and then walk along the street ahead of you, with Greenwich Market on the right. You will now be approaching the Old Royal Naval College, much of which is now used by Greenwich University. Turn right and follow this street until it reaches the gates of Greenwich Park. Don't enter the Park here though. Instead, turn right into Nevada Street and then left.

We now walk up the street called Crooms Hill. The road winds a little from side to side as we ascend and there is a story that this is connected with the name 'Crooms Hill'. Supposedly the name of this path is derived from a Celtic word meaning 'crooked' and the modern street follows the line of a footpath which predates the Roman invasion. How true this is, is anybody's guess. We might be tempted to dismiss the idea as a little piece of modern folk etymology, except that we remember the local legends about the statue in Southwark which was very ancient. It is not always wise to treat folklore and old stories too casually!

As the top of the hill is gained, it will be seen that a gate on the left gives access to Greenwich Park. If we walk through it we will see a truly extraordinary sight for which nothing can really prepare us. We are most of us aware that some parts of Britain are covered with Bronze Age and Neolithic monuments. It will come as something of a surprise to find such a landscape here, in the heart of London and with the gleaming skyscrapers of Docklands as a backdrop. Illustration 22 (see page 66) shows the view to the left of the path along which we find ourselves walking. The bumps in the grass, of which there are more than thirty, are ancient burial mounds, sometimes known as round barrows. Some of the more prominent are Anglo-Saxon, 'only' 1,500 years old. Others though are twice as old, dating back to 1000 BC or even longer ago. When the Anglo-Saxons settled in this part of England, they found that this part of the country was marked by many barrows and, perhaps thinking to stake their own claim by demonstrating continuity of custom and ritual, began interring their own dead among the existing mounds.

This area lay near Watling Street, the famous Roman road, but Watling Street had been an important track long before the coming of the Romans. It went over the higher land such as Blackheath and Shooters Hill, in order to avoid the marshy areas on the edge of the Thames. All along this part of Watling Street were prehistoric burial mounds, and one or two still exist at Woolwich Common and also Winn's Common.

We see at once an earlier iteration of the Roman custom of burying their dead in prominent places along a roadway or track. It is hard to visualize what this area was like before there were buildings and before trees had been planted to make a nice park. These barrows would have been a lot higher than they are now and also they would not have been covered with scrubby grass as they are today. Instead, they would have been gleaming white. The reason for this is that this part of London is chalkland. Rather than coming across mud or clay when we dig here, we find chalk. This means that when they were completed, these barrows would have presented an eye-catching spectacle; tall, dazzling white domes perched on top of a prominent hill which overlooked the track passing below.

It cannot be doubted that the barrows at which we are now looking are precursors of the ostentatious mausolea which were erected on Watling Street to the west of here by the Romans. The similarities are simply too great to overlook. Those who dug these barrows wanted to ensure that they would, just like those Roman tombs, be visible to any traveller passing this way. It is almost certain that both these things sprang from some common tradition which predated both the Romans and Celts.

We have talked about the very old association between Roman temples and graveyards, a tradition which continues to this day in Britain, and with the field of barrows we saw on the way to this site, it seems very likely that the nearby temple was part of that same custom. The Romans who built their temple here must have recognized something special or sacred about the land around what is now Greenwich Park.

The barrows and temple in Greenwich Park and surrounding areas demonstrate perfectly the concept at which we have been looking of the persistence of memory, the way in which a location retains an importance for successive generations or even later ethnicities or cultures. Often, the origin of a site's significance is buried so far back that we are never likely to be able to find out just what it was about some particular spot which first stirred either the imagination or religious awareness of a bunch of Neolithic hunters or Bronze Age farmers. For now, we turn our attention once more to the Roman practice of interring their dead along the roads leading into London.

The route which Watling Street took through south London is known fairly well, although there is some doubt about the original track, which, it is supposed, ran to Westminster, rather than Southwark. What we do know is that it ran through Greenwich Park and then headed along what is part of the New Cross Road. This then turns into the Old Kent Road and then Great Dover Street. It then takes a right turn and becomes Borough High Street. Along almost the entire length of this route, some four or five miles, Roman burials have been found. This seems to indicate that this was less a case of the road to Southwark passing through a cemetery, than that the whole road was regarded as some kind of extended cemetery.

Many urns containing the ashes of cremated bodies dating from the Roman occupation have turned up over the years along the Old Kent Road. Roman burials have also been uncovered to the east of Greenwich in the other direction, along Watling Street in the direction of Dover. A lead coffin was found at Plumstead. These sites are fairly scattered and the closer one gets to the city itself, the more crowded become the cluster of graves. A large number have been found in Great Dover Street, which lies between the Old Kent Road and Borough High Street, and one of these is of interest because of the light it might shed on another of the sites which we visited, that of the amphitheatre. We looked at the discovery of the supposed gladiatrix in an earlier chapter.

Chapter 14

The Decline of Londinium and the Birth of London

In the introduction to this book, it was remarked that the Roman remains in the city are chiefly found underground now, due to the fact that the street level has risen over the centuries. This is not of course the whole explanation, because in Rome itself the 2,000-year-old past is still there for all to see. Buildings such as the Pantheon, together with the monumental arch of Constantine, Trajan's Column and almost the whole of the forum stand as tall as they did at the height of the Roman Empire. Clearly, some other factor must have been at work in London to bring about the sorry state of affairs there. After all, London once boasted the mightiest basilica north of the Alps. What happened to it?

We have looked at 400 years or so of Roman history in the capital of Britain. It may perhaps be fitting to end our examination of this subject with an account of how Londinium came to an end and what happened in the next century or so. This will also explain how some of the buildings at which we have looked, such as the basilica and forum, and the public baths at Huggin Hill, came to be ruins. Much of this happened even before the Romans abandoned London and although we cannot know the details for sure, it is nevertheless an interesting story.

The fortunes of Londinium rose and fell over the centuries and with them, the fabric of the city grew and shrank. There were booms and slumps, rebellions and retribution, war and invasion. All these things had an effect upon the city and left their mark. Sometimes, the mark which they made was negative, in that landmarks were removed or deliberately demolished. This happened with that enormous basilica. As we saw in Chapter 2, the only visible part of this is now a stump of masonry, hidden away in the basement of a hairdresser. What happened to the rest of it? Where did the forum go? Why was the public bathhouse at Huggin Hill demolished? Although this book is really a guide to archaeological remains, rather than a history book, it might perhaps interest readers to know why those few fragments of the city are all that can now be seen of Londinium.

When looking at history, we like to see clear and distinct narratives, where we are able to see cause and effect and the whole jumble of facts is coherent and makes some kind of sense. So it is that we think of the Roman invasion of Britain and an occupation lasting 400 years, until the Romans left and the Saxons arrived. Then, 600 years later, came the Norman Conquest. This is fine for children's books, but it is not really how things happened in real life, and it is the forgotten stories of what really happened in the later years of the Roman occupation which explain what really happened to the fabric of the city which we have explored in the course of this book.

Let us start with the 450ft-long basilica which, together with a forum, stood on Cornhill. A reconstruction may be seen in Illustration 8 (see page 21). What happened to it? Was it simply abandoned when the Romans left and then pulled to pieces by those who wished to use its stones for new buildings? It was, after all, a very large building, almost as long as, and probably as sturdily constructed as, the modern St Paul's Cathedral. The answer is that by the time the Roman city fell into decay, the basilica had not been around for 150 years. It was systematically demolished, by the Romans themselves, in around 300 AD.

There are two principal theories relating to the destruction of the basilica. One is that the population of Londinium had shrunk so much by this time, for various reasons, that the maintenance and upkeep of so huge a town hall, with all its attendant offices for the administration of a thriving city which was not as important as it had once been, was simply too much. By this reading of the situation, the basilica, which had once been a proud symbol of the great significance of the city in the scheme of things, was by 300 AD a white elephant. The expense could no longer be justified and so it was knocked down. The other possibility is that the dismantling of the basilica was a punishment inflicted on Londinium for being the base of an adventurer who tried to usurp the position of emperor of Rome. The story is an interesting one and leads on naturally to an explanation of why the bastions were constructed along the eastern part of the city wall in the latter half of the fourth century AD.

In the late third century AD, a Roman naval commander whose ancestral origins lay in what is now France rather than Rome itself had control of a fleet of ships in the North Sea and the English Channel. His job was to chase off the increasingly bold incursions made by Saxons and others from what is now northern Germany. Sometimes, the Saxons attacked shipping, but at other times they launched audacious raids upon the coast of Britain and Roman settlements in other parts of Europe. This man, Carausius, was a very cunning and duplicitous character. He struck deals with the Saxon pirates so that he shared the profits of their activities, and this netted Carausius and his men a good income. When the emperor of Rome, Maximian, heard of this, he sentenced Carausius to death. Nothing daunted, Carausius took his fleet to Britain, seized London and declared himself Emperor of Britain and Gaul. So feeble was Roman power at this time that for the next five years Carausius ruled Britain from his base in Londinium. He was eventually murdered in around 302 AD by one of his commanders, called Allectus, who then assumed power and ruled for another three years.

As the old saying has it though, all good things come to an end and a new emperor, Constantius, decided that the time had come to put an end to the pretensions of the man who was now styling himself 'emperor'. In 305 AD, Constantius gathered an army and invaded Britain. Allectus brought his army, which included many mercenaries from Northern Europe, south to meet the emperor in battle. The ragtag army of Allectus was no match for that of Constantius and his troops were scattered. Seeing that the game was more or less up, many of them fled to London and began pillaging the city, hoping to steal what they could and cause as much damage to the place as possible. When Constantius arrived in London with his army, he put an end to this and a famous commemorative medallion was minted, showing the grateful citizens of London thanking the emperor for saving their city from ruin.

The reality though was that Constantius was more than a little annoyed with the British and especially those living in the capital city. For eight years they had consented to live under men who had usurped the power of Rome. It is suggested that the emperor ordered the destruction of the basilica and forum as a punishment for their acquiescence in what amounted to a rebellion against the authority of Rome. By destroying the largest building in Europe north of the Alps, Constantius intended to humiliate Londoners and show them the price to be paid by those who revolted.

It has to be said that this is a more plausible explanation of the destruction of the basilica by Roman forces in the early fourth century than the idea that it was no longer needed. If that was the case, why not simply abandon it, rather than going to the immense trouble of pulling it down? The pile of rubble and ruinous walls which were left after the demolition would hardly have been an attractive sight in the city. If the idea was though to teach Londoners a lesson for harbouring traitors and rebels, then those ruins would be a daily reminder of the price to be paid for such actions.

The dismantling of the bathhouse at Huggin Hill though, is a different matter. The baths flourished for a century or more and then, some time in the second century AD, fell into disuse. They were then partially torn down and the building materials used elsewhere. This might be because the population of London was declining in the third century. There had been a great fire in around 130 AD and after this, there are indications that the city never really regained its vitality. In some places, previously built-up areas were covered with a layer of dark earth, as though they had been turned over to cultivation, perhaps as gardens or allotments.

In 367 AD, came the dramatic incident known as the Barbarian Conspiracy, evidence for which may be seen in the construction of the bastions which have been mentioned, such as the example which is shown in Illustration 35 (see page 98). After Constantius defeated Allectus and restored Britain to its proper place as a province of the Roman Empire, London enjoyed for 50 or 60 years something very much like a golden age of peace and prosperity. This was not to last though.

Throughout the fourth century AD, the Saxons and Franks grew stronger and more vigorous, as the Roman Empire became weaker and less able. This is of course only evident in retrospect. For those living at the time, it only became obvious when an alarming event took place which revealed just how feeble the once mighty empire was becoming. In 367 AD, some of those serving on the borders of Britain in Wales and near Scotland were foreigners who owed little genuine allegiance to Rome. That autumn, they abandoned their posts at Hadrian's Wall and allowed the Picts to sweep south across the border. At the same time, probably as part of a coordinated strategy, landings were made in what is now Wales from Ireland and Saxons attacked the south-east coast of Britain. This is why the affair became known as the Barbarian Conspiracy and also the Great Conspiracy, because it was clear that various tribes and nations were all acting in concert against the province. That winter, the barbarian hordes ran wild across much of Britain, looting and pillaging at will. It was a grim time for the British, especially those living in isolated villas near the coast or the border with Scotland.

This would have been a pretty unpleasant winter for the Romanized inhabitants of Britain and it was not until the following spring that Roman authority was re-established by an expedition from the Continent. It was after this episode that the bastions were added to the city wall, and this is the reason that almost all of them were built on that part of the wall which faces east. It was from that direction, nearest to the east coast of Britain, that raiders who had landed from Northern

Europe would be likely to arrive at the walls of the capital. At about the same time, frantic efforts were being made to reinforce the riverside wall which protected Londinium from attack by ships sailing up the Thames. The parts of the wall along the waterfront which had been built before this had fairly solid foundations. After 367 AD though, the wall was strengthened by taking blocks of statuary from temples and pieces of a monumental archway and simply ramming them into the clay of the riverbank. Illustration 28 (see page 80) shows a part of this wall, which is made up of different types of stone, varying greatly in size. It is very different from the neat workmanship of the earlier landward city wall. Illustration 59 is of a carving showing four mother goddesses, which was simply taken from a temple and placed on the riverside.

We see now, perhaps, one of the reasons why London is a little lacking in large structures dating from the Roman occupation. At

59. An altar reused for building of the riverside wall.

one time, there were a number of temples in London, together with monumental arches. When there grew a desperate fear of attack by the Saxons, either by water from the Thames or overland from Essex and Kent after having landed on the coast, then the need for defences at all costs trumped every other consideration. The riverside wall was constructed, using altars and statuary, while at the same time, thousands of tons of stone was needed to build the bastions along the eastern side of the city wall. When buildings were being pulled down to supply extra material for the walls, it should not come as any surprise that it is the city walls which endured, rather than the temples and graveyards.

Between 383 and 410 AD, there was increasing chaos and disorder in the empire. At one point, the commander of forces in Britain declared himself emperor and ruled the country for a while and in Rome itself, there was murder and intrigue and successive emperors faced both rival claimants for the throne, as well as increasingly determined incursions from territories north of the Rhine. In Britain, the Picts were making seaborne raids and the Saxons were able to operate with impunity in the North Sea. By 410 AD, matters had reached a climax, both for Britain and the Roman Empire. In that year, the city of Rome itself was sacked by the Visigoths and Britain appealed for assistance to defend itself against the Saxons and Picts. Emperor Honorius told the leaders of Britain that they would have to make provision for their own defence and that they could expect no further aid from Rome.

How did all these dramatic developments affect London? It used to be thought that they signalled a rapid decline in the city's fortunes and the quality of life for those living there, but there is some reason to suppose that life continued much as usual for at least some Londoners well into the fifth century. In an earlier chapter, we discussed the house in Billingsgate and learned that it had a hypocaust. When archaeologists cleared away the wood ash from the last time that the furnace of the hypocaust had been in use, they found beneath it part of an amphora, which has been thought to have been imported in the first decades of the fifth century. This indicates that those in the house were still living in the Roman style, even after Rome had officially disavowed responsibility for the province of Britain. Within a few years though, the roof had fallen in and by about 450 AD somebody had lost a distinctively Saxon brooch in the ruins of the house.

By the end of the fourth century AD, it was probably clear to many people that the Roman Empire was not what it had once been and the shrewder and more far-sighted could perhaps see that it might not be too long before it disintegrated entirely. With the pressures growing on its borders in mainland Europe, it was perhaps dawning on people in Britain that they could not rely forever on the protection of the Roman army from marauders, pirates and irregular forces arriving from the Continent. The process of the collapse of Roman civilization was slow, but inexorable. For some reason, the Saxons and Vikings had no desire actually to live in the decaying walled city. They were happy enough to loot the place and carry off any building materials which they felt might be useful, but there was perhaps some kind of taboo on actually living in the old place. Instead, a new port was established further upstream, in the area around what is now Covent Garden and the Strand. This was called Lundenwic.

What was it about the old walled city which made it an unattractive place to live? We cannot be sure, but a poem written during the Saxon period might offer a clue. The poem, called *The Ruin*, is about a deserted Roman city;

> Well-wrought this wall-stone, weird broke it:
> Bastions busted, burst is giant's work,
> Roofs are ruined, ruptured turrets,
> Ring-gate broken, rime on lime-work
> Cloven shower-shields, sheered, fallen.
> Age ate under them. Earth-grasp holds fast.
> The noble workers, decayed, departed,
> In earth's hard grip, while a hundred times,
> The generations pass.

There is a sadness about this description, mingled with a sense of awe. The phrase 'giant's work' suggests that there was felt to be something uncanny or supernatural about the ruins of such cities. It was not surprising then that few people wished to linger in them after nightfall.

They may not have wanted to live in Londinium, but the Saxons were happy to set up churches there. The earliest buildings still standing which were built after the fall of Roman London are both churches. One of these is All Hallows by the Tower, which was erected on the site of a Roman house. In about 650 AD, the first incarnation of this church was built, using the remains of the nearby Roman buildings. We can see some of the Saxon stonework in the crypt of All Hallows, but most astonishingly, there still stands the only Saxon arch in the whole of London. This may be seen in Illustration 43 (see page 114) and it will at once be observed that the arch is constructed of Roman tiles, scavenged from the ruins which must at that time have abounded.

In the crypt of St Bride's church in Fleet Street is some masonry which is said to be even older than this; about 100 years older. Some time in the sixth century, a building was erected on the site of St Bride's. Unfortunately, whoever the builders were, they were unaware of the previous Roman digging in this area, which, for reasons at which we can only guess, involved a large trench or ditch. Over the years, this had become filled with all kinds of rubbish, which had the effect of making it a good deal less solid than the rest of the ground nearby. The Saxons started building and were ill-advised enough to place one corner of their structure over the rubbish-filled ditch. It was not long before the walls cracked, proving that subsidence was a problem even in 550 AD. Only a small part of one corner of this structure can still be seen in the crypt; on the right-hand side after coming down the stairs.

There were two exceptions to the general rule of not living within the walls of the abandoned city. The Church in Rome, perhaps because of some lingering sense of imperialism, thought that they needed to deal with Londinium when communicating with the British churches. It was for this reason that St Paul's, on the western of the two hills upon which the city was founded, became the most important church in the whole country. This situation still exists of course; the cathedral in London has always been the heart of Christianity in Britain, notwithstanding the fact that the most important Anglican bishop in the country is Archbishop not of London, but of Canterbury.

There was also a royal palace inside the walls of London during the Saxon period, although where it by have been is anybody's guess. The Guildhall is built above the north side of the amphitheatre, which was traditionally where the dignitaries and important spectators sat. It has been suggested that this fact is of some significance, and that this was where the folkmoot once assembled, in the old arena, with the leaders of the people on the northern side. This though is only guesswork and we are never likely to know for sure.

For the better part of 400 years then, Londinium was more or less deserted and the stones and tiles carried off for building work elsewhere. Then, towards the end of the ninth century, the depredations of the Vikings sailing up the river reached such a level as to cause those living in Lundenwic to view the old walled city with new eyes. It was certainly a more defensible site than the trading port along the banks of the river where the Strand is now. So it was that an ancient taboo was overcome and a Saxon city rose in the long-abandoned ruins of Roman London. We have King Alfred to thank for this move.

Of course, the walled city was not altogether abandoned and empty, even if the majority of the population of this part of the Thames Valley was to be found further upstream in Lundenwic. We know that at least one church had already been standing within the walls for a couple of centuries when Alfred re-established the place as a stronghold. This was All Hallows by the Tower, at whose Saxon arch we have already looked. We also saw, in the chapter on Roman roads, the way in which the street plan of modern London shows clearly the influence of the Roman roads and walls, and it has also been mentioned that the Saxons too influenced the layout of the City of London in several places. Perhaps it will do no harm to remind readers of these, as they can now be set in their proper context of the return of life to the largely ruinous and abandoned Roman city.

When the settlement of Lundenwic was thriving, around what is now Covent Garden and the Strand, travellers and traders wishing to reach it from the east of England still travelled along the 'Great Road', the one which stretches up into Essex and passed through Ilford, Romford and other places between London and Colchester. Using this Roman road, which although no doubt dilapidated and overgrown with weeds by that time, was still easier than trekking overland and it ran straight to the old city. Once travellers reached Aldgate, they very likely found it tiresome and pointless to walk around the walls of the city to continue on their way to Lundenwic. There may have been some kind of taboo on living among the ruins of the city, but presumably this did not prevent anybody from using it as a short cut to get from Aldgate to Ludgate, where another Roman road led to Lundenwic.

Getting from Aldgate to Ludgate, those crossing the city would have found their way blocked by the remains of the basilica and forum. Although these had been demolished hundreds of years earlier, the foundations remained, as indeed they do to this very day, beneath Leadenhall Market. So it was that they skirted around the forum to the south, making a new path through what remained of Londinium. Since there was presumably a good deal of traffic between what we now know as East Anglia and the new town of Lundenwic, it is likely that some efforts were made to clear the route through the walled city a little, by removing stones and making the way clear. This new road can still be seen to this day in the curving path which Fenchurch Street and Lombard Street adopt as they pass south of what was the forum. It is plain that these streets, which are based upon the ancient road which once ran here, deliberately avoid the site of the forum and basilica.

Returning for a moment to the subject of the Guildhall and its supposed connection with later Saxon folkmoots, it is an undeniable fact that when the medieval streets took shape in the city, they often followed the Saxon layout. This is remarkably clear if one looks closely at a large-scale map of the area around the Guildhall. It will at once be seen that what was once the arena of the amphitheatre is still, thousands of years later, an open space. To the south, Gresham Street bulges out strangely, for no apparent reason, causing the church of St Lawrence Jewry to be set at an awkward angle to the Guildhall which it faces. To the east and west of the open space, the streets of Aldermanbury and Basinghall Street both flare out around the Guildhall and the space in front of it. Clearly, in Saxon times and then the medieval period, there was something special about that area which meant that it was not built on and nor did roads cut across it.

We have reached the end of our exploration of Roman London, because although it was more or less abandoned and, technically perhaps, still Londinium until the late ninth century AD, from that time onwards, it acquired a new name. The earliest traces of the reoccupation of the walled city date from around 870–880 AD. When it was inhabited again, none of those now living there felt inclined to call the place by its Roman name, even assuming that they might have known it. The settlement by the Strand had been known as Lundenwic, because 'wic' meant 'village'. That's really all that the little port was, a village. But once they had set up their homes in the old walled city, the case was altered. This was a defensible position, established on hilltops. So it was that a new name was chosen for the changed situation. The place was to become known as Lundenburg. This signalled the final break with the past and Londinium was now no more than part of history.

Just in case it should seem to anybody that all this is ancient history, with no conceivable relevance for the modern world, it is worth ending with a reflection on how the city of Londinium affected the modern world. We still talk about the 'square mile' or the 'City', to refer to that part of the capital which was once the walled city of the Romans. That this area was a centre for finance and trade is still indicated in our name for it. Whenever we hear or read of the mood 'in the City', we know at once that business and finance is the topic. This then is an echo which has reverberated through the last couple of thousand years. It is an implicit recognition that the City of London, the heart of British financial affairs, is still recognized as the trading hub of Britain.

Chapter 15

How Roman London became Forgotten

When first I suggested this book to my publisher, the response was a little dubious. The grounds for this hesitation were very simple and practical; surely there were not enough Roman remains in London to justify an entire book on the subject? Where on earth would I find the material which would allow people a chance of exploring Roman London? It is to be hoped that readers might feel otherwise by this point. This feeling though, that there are few traces to be seen of the Roman occupation in the capital, is a very common one. A lot of people have heard that there is a bit of the old city wall near the Tower of London, and a few even remember hearing that part an amphitheatre was dug up 30 or 40 years ago, but that is about it. Even then, there is doubt as to the age of the wall at Tower Hill. Some people assume that it is medieval, rather than Roman. About the other things at which we have been looking, there is an almost complete lack of awareness. When I tell people that the foundations of the turrets and parts of the walls of a Roman fort are open to view by any passer-by, they look at me in frank disbelief. The news that a visit to a London church can entail walking across the floor of a Roman house is something which not one Londoner in 10,000 knows about.

What is the cause of this ignorance about the Roman origins of London and the visible signs of the presence of the conquerors which are openly displayed in the modern city? Many cities are proud of their most ancient remains and do their best to publicize them but in London, Roman history seems to be something of a hole and corner affair, so that those wishing to learn about the subject are obliged to go to a dozen different sources for information. Why should it be that the very oldest structures in the capital are overlooked in this way? To answer this question, we need to consider the psychology of the matter.

In Athens, the citizens are able to look with some satisfaction and pride on the ancient columns and temples. These, after all, were produced by their own ancestors, when most people in Europe were still living in mud huts. In Rome too, the forum has been preserved and partially reconstructed. It is the glory of the city and one of the first ports of call for any tourist. This too, is something of which the inhabitants of modern Rome may be justly proud. Thousands of years ago, their forebears were able to produce this enduring and spectacular site. How different, how very different, has the approach of Londoners been. In the heart of London, beneath Leadenhall Market and Cornhill, are the remains of a huge Roman forum, the concrete foundations of which still endure. When the Victorians were building in that area during the nineteenth century, they could, instead of building a marketplace, have uncovered the forum and restored it to view. The foundations of the basilica were also there; the largest building north of the Alps at the time of the Roman Empire. Instead, the workmen were ordered to set to with pickaxes and hammer, or gunpowder when these would not serve, and to destroy as much of the remains of the basilica and forum as possible, before burying them beneath blocks of offices and a huge market. Why were the forums of London and Rome treated so very differently? Those wishing to see the last fragment of the basilica available to view, now have to descend the stairs of a hairdresser and peer into a glass case. Rather than a tourist attraction, our own basilica and forum are hidden away as though they are an embarrassment.

What then accounts for this different attitude to the earliest remains of the capital cities of Britain, Italy and Greece? The most obvious is of course that for us in Britain, Roman sites are a reminder that we were not always a mighty empire and world power, but that in a sense, civilization was brought to these islands by another nation. That is a sobering thought and the implications are perhaps more profound than at first appear. Nobody likes to be reminded that their country was colonized and occupied by a foreign power. We only have to see the current fuss about 'decolonization' to see how touchy people can be about this. Those whose territories were colonized by the British find the memory of such events humiliating. Colonization casts a long shadow, even if, as in the case of the British Empire, we are only looking back a century or two. For the British, even the idea of living in towns was a novelty imposed upon them by foreigners.

This distaste for the idea of having once been subservient to another European country is a long-standing one and it led in the Middle Ages to the publication of the first book of British history, which succeeded in devising an entire mythos which neatly circumvented the need to feel degraded by having been colonized by Rome. When Geoffrey of Monmouth's *Historia Regum Brittanniae* ('History of the Kings of Britain') was published in Oxford in 1135, it managed to create for this country a grand history which proved that far from being a bunch of savages when the Romans came, Britain had at that time a classical civilization which actually predated that of Rome.

Nothing could be more calculated to appeal to British pride than learning that in 1170 BC, a Trojan prince had defeated a race of giants who were living here and established a dynasty from which we are all descended. According to Geoffrey, after the destruction of Troy, which we read of in Homer's *Iliad*, a prince called Aeneas escaped from the city by sea and went in search of a new realm. This was of course simply lifted from Virgil's *Aeneid*. Geoffrey then carries on the story by inventing a great-grandson called Brutus for Aeneas, one who is given a heroic destiny. The goddess Diana appears to him in a dream and makes a prophecy, saying;

> Brutus, beyond the setting of the sun, past the realms of Gaul there lies an island in the sea, once occupied by giants. Now it is empty and ready for your folk. Down the years this will prove an abode suited to you and to your people: and for your

descendants it will be a second Troy. A race of kings will be
born there from your stock and the round circle of the whole
earth will be subject to them.

This was heartening news indeed for the British in the twelfth century
and it is little wonder that for the next 400 or 500 years, the *Historia*
was regarded as the best source to learn about the origins of the people
of Britain. It seemed that Brutus, the exiled Trojan prince, gave his
name to Britain and that it was he and not the Romans who founded
London. After clearing out and defeating the last of the giants who
were living in Britain when he arrived, Brutus decided to build a city.
He arrived at the Thames and then built a city which he named *Troia
Nova* or New Troy. This is supposedly the origin of the name of the
Trinovantes, a tribe of Celts living in southern Britain at the time of
the Roman invasion.

A big attraction of the *Historia* was that it demoted the Romans
and showed that they were not such a big influence on Britain after all.
Rather than coming to the Thames Valley and finding a deserted piece
of marshland that they managed to turn into a fine city, they arrived
to find that a city had already been established in that spot a thousand
years earlier. The city of Bath, which was of course an entirely Roman
creation, was also given a back story. Geoffrey of Monmouth wrote
that it had been built by King Bladud in about 900 BC. It was already
ancient when the Romans turned up there. Bladud was given a son,
Lear, and his three daughters around whom Shakespeare wrote the
play *King Lear*.

All this, which was almost certainly dreamed up in the main by
Geoffrey, was very encouraging to British people, leading them to
believe for centuries that London was older than Rome. One final
example might be amusing. From the name Ludgate, Geoffrey
dreamed up a King Lud, who before the Romans set foot in Britain,
're-built the walls of the town of Trinovantum and girded it round with
innumerable towers'. We learn that the town was later named Kaerlud

after the king, but that this was later corrupted to Kaerlundein and then London for short. The Romans receive short thrift from Geoffrey, being driven out of Britain by a Cornish King called Asclepiodotus. By the time of the Tudors in the late sixteenth century, the Romans had been reduced to the role of bit-players in British history and all the important figures of the distant past were imaginary heroes with Trojan origins.

It may seem that we have veered wildly off the topic of why the average person living in London in the early twenty-first century knows little about the many remains to be seen of the Roman city, but a moment's thought will show that this is not really so. Geoffrey of Monmouth allowed the people of London to delude themselves for hundreds of years that a thousand years before the Romans arrived, there was a fabulous classical city, looking something like Athens perhaps, where Londinium began. Far from coming and civilizing us, the Romans actually debased a people whose noble history stretched back further than that of Rome, a people moreover who had a divine destiny to rule the world. One is irresistibly reminded of the line from the Western *The Man Who Shot Liberty Valance*; 'When the legend becomes fact, print the legend'. So it was that the British preferred to print the legend when it came to the origins of their nation. This entailed forgetting about the Romans and concentrating more on the legendary heroes and kings of their own country.

It was the nineteenth century which saw the wholesale destruction of much of what remained of Londinium. At a time when some countries in Europe were beginning to capitalize on their history and preserve the past so that it could be seen forever, the British appeared keen to eradicate all trace of London's past. Perhaps one can understand this, because of course this was the height of empire, a time when the sun never set on Britain's colonies. One can readily appreciate why nobody would want to dwell on the fact that their own capital had been founded by foreigners and that for centuries, they had been no more than a colony themselves. The Roman walls and foundations which kept turning up as the Victorians turned their capital into a thoroughly modern metropolis for the age of steam and telegraphs must have been an uncomfortable reminder that all kingdoms and empires ultimately end in dust. This is not something of which a vigorous, dynamic and expanding world power wishes to be reminded.

So it was that every time a chunk of Roman London came to light, it was either blown up or smashed to pieces. The sheer quantity of the remains which were ruthlessly disposed of at that time is amazing. Looking at the illustrated newspapers of the time shows many Roman remains which were found and promptly demolished. In Chapter 7 we passed Goldsmiths' Hall, on the junction of Foster Lane and Gresham Street. When the foundations for this building were being dug in 1830, massive masonry footings were found, which could have been the podium for a Roman temple. So strong were these that gunpowder was resorted to and they were blow to pieces. Nothing was allowed to impede the progress of London in those days, certainly not some old bits of stone from the distant past.

Something of this feeling which the Victorians had for Roman London lingers on to this day. Tourists who leave Tower Hill Tube station make a beeline for the Tower of London, which is, they think, the only old thing worth stopping to look at in this part of London. Many of them hurry by the 35ft-high wall, with some of the best examples of Roman masonry in Britain, without even noticing it. The more perfectly preserved length of wall a few yards away, which even has all the original red sandstone plinth intact is literally never visited by tourists, or indeed anybody else. A short walk from here too is the church of All Hallows by the Tower, which we visited when seeing what Roman homes were like. There is a Roman floor across which visitors can walk. A stone's throw away is the Billingsgate Roman house and bathhouse. None of these places though attract either tourists or Londoners themselves.

It is almost as though the slight sense of shame which was once felt in London about the idea of being occupied by a bunch of foreigners who even founded our very capital city, lingers on and causes us subconsciously to avoid thinking of them. Westminster Abbey, Buckingham Palace and St Paul's Cathedral are all landmarks of which we may be justly proud, they were produced by our own ancestors. Those alien city walls though, with their weird horizontal red stripes, these are part of somebody else's culture and heritage. No wonder that we have knocked down most of them and hide the rest away so that it requires great ingenuity to track down what remains above ground.

An example of how this process is still at work today, even when somebody is actually seeking out Roman remains, might perhaps be instructive. As we have seen, the site of only one Roman temple is accessible and open to view in modern London. This is the one in Greenwich Park. While writing this book, I visited the place where the temple once stood and was shocked to discover that a section of flooring which had once stood here, surrounded by railings, had been removed. It was there in 2011, but it has now vanished, possibly as a result of the use of the park during the 2012 Olympic Games. A visit to the Greenwich Visitors Centre in the Old Royal Naval College which is near the station, was interesting. There is a small museum here with displays of armour and statuary from the time of Henry VIII. There was no sign though of the finds from the temple. When I asked those working there, they had no idea what I was talking about. Indeed, they did not even know that there *was* a Roman site a few hundred yards away. Attempts to find out where the material found at the temple have been fruitless and nobody seems to know why the Roman floor was ripped up and removed. What is curious is that it is now certain that there are traces of other buildings near the temple and it seems likely that this was not just a single temple, but a complex of connected buildings. It would surely be possible to recreate a Romano-Celtic religious sanctuary in this part of the park, but there appears to be no inclination on anybody's part to do so. This reluctance or disinclination to properly explore the Roman site in Greenwich Park is all the more puzzling after the exceptionally hot and dry summer of 2022. As the grass withered, the line of the Roman walls became clearly delineated and the ghostly outline of the temple emerged.

In case it might be thought that I have exaggerated the case about the avoidance of the Roman history of Britain, readers might like to try a little experiment, which entails searching Amazon for books on Roman London and then repeating the process only this time looking for books on the Tudor city. The few Roman books are mainly hugely expensive academic studies and a few second-hand copies of popular books from the 1980s. This is very different from what we find when we look for stuff about Tudor London. There is no doubt that, for whatever reason, we are less apt to wish to hear about, look at the remains of or read books on Roman London than any other period in in the city' history. It is to be hoped that this present book will serve to balance this a little and encourage people to treat Roman London as a subject worth investigating.

A final word might be fitting, because there are some recent signs that the remembrance of Roman Britain might be becoming slightly more popular in the last year or two for a very peculiar reason. There are persistent, but wholly unsubstantiated, stories that Roman Britain was a very multicultural society, with black people mingling on equal terms with white Romans and Celts. This is an attractive idea for those who wish to demonstrate that black people have always lived in this country. Although this is a dubious hypothesis, it fits in very well with the spirit of modern Britain, and Roman society in Britain is now being held up as an example of multiracial harmony. The Museum of London, which had some excellent reconstructions of domestic interiors in Roman London, will be reopening on another site in 2026 and it has already been decided that the new display of life in Roman London will centre around a fictional character called Ulpia, who is, it seems, a young, black single mother. It is she who has been chosen as the supposed householder who owns the new Roman house that is to be recreated. In this way, the Roman history of Britain might perhaps be rehabilitated, focusing less upon the fact that it reduced Britain to the status of a colony and more on the idea that the Romans were enlightened about some very modern ideas and could teach us a thing or two about tolerance. Ulpia's children, for instance, are shown to be mixed-race. It may be that fantasies of this kind will achieve the purpose of reviving interest in the study of Roman London.

Appendix: The Sights of Roman London

This purpose of this appendix is to provide readers with a list of the sites and recovered artifacts mentioned in this book, with postcodes and, where possible, telephone numbers, websites and email addresses.

The Amphitheatre
The Guildhall Art Gallery
Guildhall Yard
London EC2V 5AE
Telephone 020 7332 3700
Email guildhall.artgallery@cityoflondon.gov.uk

Billingsgate House and Baths
101 Lower Thames Street
London EC32 6DL
Email billingsgatebathhouse@cityoflondon.gov.uk

Roman house and pavement
All Hallows by the Tower
Byward Street
London EC3R 5BJ
Telephone 020 7481 2928
Website http://www.allhallowsbythetower.org.uk/

Supporting wall of Huggin Hill Bathhouse
Cleary Garden

Queen Victoria Street
London EC4V 2AR
Telephone 020 7374 4127

Roman road
Southwark Cathedral
London Bridge
London
Telephone 020 7367 6700
Email cathedral@southwark.anglican.org

The fort
Noble Street
London EC2

Roman floor
St Bride's Church
Fleet Street
London EC4Y 8AU
Telephone 020 7427 0133
Email stb@stbrides.com

Timber from the first Roman bridge or wharf
St Magnus the Martyr
Lower Thames Street
London EC3R 6DN
Telephone 020 7626 4481
Website https://www.stmagnusmartyr.org.uk/contact/

Site of Romano-Celtic Temple
Greenwich Park
Greenwich Park Office
Blackheath Gate

Charlton Way
Greenwich
London SE10 8QY
Telephone 0300 061 2380
Email https://www.royalparks.org.uk/about-us/contact-us

Temple of Mithras
12 Walbrook
London EC4N 8AA
Email info@londonmithraeum.com

Crofton Roman Villa
Crofton Road
Orpington
Kent BR6 8AF
Email crofton.roman.villa@gmail.com

Part of the Basilica
Nicholson & Griffin
90 Gracechurch Street
Leadenhall Market
London EC3V 0DN
Telephone 07380 518683

Statue of Minerva
Trinity Church Square
London SE1

Visible Sections of the Roman City Wall
Platform of Tower Hill Tube Station
Trinity Square
London EC3N 4DJ

Tower Hill Garden
London EC3N 4DJ

8–11 Crescent
London EC3

1 America Square
London EC3N 2LS

35 Vine Street
London EC3N 2PX

Bay 52
London Wall Car Park
23 London Wall
London EC2V 5DY

St Alphage Garden, off London Wall
London EC2Y 5EL

St Giles Cripplegate Church
4 The Postern, Barbican,
London EC2Y 8BJ

Bank of America Merrill Lynch Financial Centre
2 King Edward Street
London EC1A 1HQ
Telephone 020 7628 1000

The River Wall
The Tower of London
London EC3N 4AB

Index